THE
RACQUETBALL
BOOK

THE
RACQUETBALL
BOOK

by
Steve Strandemo
and
Bill Bruns

Photographs by Jack Miller

PUBLISHED BY POCKET BOOKS NEW YORK

THE RACQUETBALL BOOK

POCKET BOOK edition published October, 1977

This original POCKET BOOK edition is printed from brand-new plates. POCKET BOOK editions are published by
POCKET BOOKS,
a Simon & Schuster Division of
GULF & WESTERN CORPORATION
1230 Avenue of the Americas,
New York, N.Y. 10020.
Trademarks registered in the United States
and other countries.

ISBN: 0-671-81712-4
Copyright, © 1977, by Steve Strandemo and Bill Bruns.
Published by POCKET BOOKS, New York.

Interior design by Laura Bernay

Printed in the U.S.A.

To my editor, Marty Asher, whose confidence and enthusiasm made this book a reality.

To the special people who took part in those arduous photography sessions: Jack, Linda, Terry, Harvey, and Pauly.

To all the racquetball players I've watched play—from novice to top professional, women and men alike—who have given me the knowledge to write this book.

CONTENTS

THE
RACQUETBALL
BOOK

INTRODUCTION

Racquetball is a challenging, fast-moving game that combines some of the best features of tennis, handball, squash, badminton—and simple mayhem. Yet we can all enjoy it at the competitive level we seek. Men, women, and children can play one another in singles, cutthroat, and doubles, and whoever has a proper sense of strategy and a few basic shots can hold his or her own against an opponent with greater power or experience. Moreover, an hour of energetic play will give you all the exercise you can handle; the game will keep you fit, or get you into better shape. In fact, *The West Point Fitness and Diet Book* rates racquetball among the top four lifetime sports in promoting overall physical fitness—the others being bicycling, swimming, and handball.

Another important reason for racquetball's popularity is that whatever your age, and whatever your "natural" athletic abilities, you can enjoy the sport to the fullest—and learn to play it right.

Racquetball is played on an enclosed court, 20 feet wide, 40 feet long, and 20 feet high, with the ceiling very much in play. You swing what resembles a scaled-down tennis racquet, and you hit a lively black or green rubber ball (red and blue balls are also coming on the market).

Play begins with one person serving from the service zone, usually near the middle of the court. His or her opponent must stand at least five feet behind the back service line, or "short" line, but the normal ready position is about two steps off the back wall.

The server is allowed two serves. He or she bounces the ball and then

The racquet and the ball used in racquetball

must hit it directly to the front wall. If the ball strikes a side wall, floor, or ceiling before hitting the front wall, the server loses serve. All other errors on the first serve simply result in a fault, and the server receives a final attempt, as in tennis.

If the ball strikes the front wall correctly, then it must rebound beyond the short line in order to be in play—but without hitting the back wall in the air before touching the floor. The ball can ricochet off one of the side walls coming back from the front wall, but two side-wall hits is a fault.

The service returner cannot hit the ball until it passes the short line, and then he must contact the ball before it bounces twice on the floor. Contact is usually made on the first bounce, but it will sometimes occur in the air against softly hit lob serves. The receiver can use any combination of walls (including the ceiling) in returning the ball to the front wall, provided the ball doesn't first hit the floor, called a "skip."

If the ball strikes the front wall legally, then the rally continues until one player fails to return the ball before it bounces on the floor twice, or the shot "skips" before reaching the front wall. Points are scored only to the serving player (or side in doubles) when the server wins the rally or serves an "ace." The first player to reach 21 points wins the game. Matches are generally two out of three games, with the final game often played to 11 or 15, depending on the standards used—and the shape you and your opponent are in.

An important part of racquetball's appeal is the way it brings out a person's best competitive instincts at every level. For example, beginners

Play begins with the server hitting the ball from near the middle of the service zone. His opponent positions herself about two strides from the back wall, ready to break toward either side of the court.

Court Dimensions and Markings

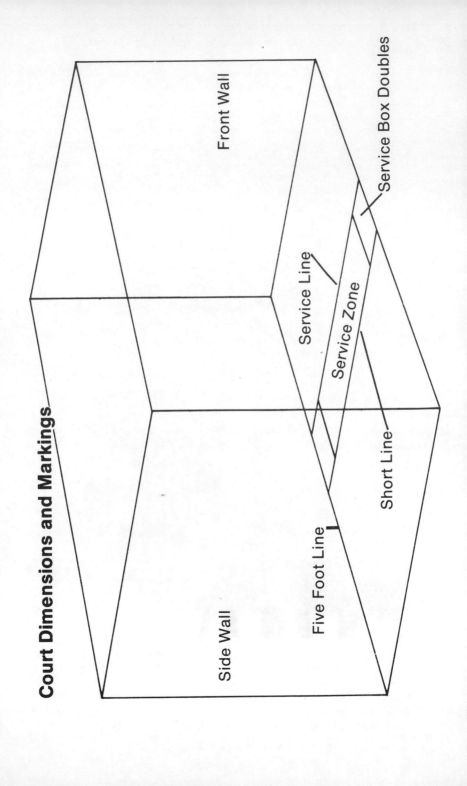

Front Wall

Service Box Doubles

Service Line

Service Zone

Short Line

Five Foot Line

Side Wall

find that racquetball is easier to learn and much less intimidating to play than tennis. The racquet is smaller and easier to control; the stroking techniques produce less frustration in the early learning stages; and you have more leeway for error. Shots that would be errors in tennis usually rebound off a side wall or the ceiling and hit the front wall, thus keeping the rally alive. In short, virtually every person can achieve "instant mediocrity" in the privacy of a four-wall room. The angle at which the ball ricochets off these walls is confusing at first, but if you can take this bouncing ball and hit the broad side of a barn from about 30 feet away, you can play a match—and have a lot of fun—the first time you step on the court.

Pretty soon, however, since "mediocrity" is so easily attained, most players discover that the real challenge and enjoyment of racquetball is derived from the effort to play the game properly; to cover the court efficiently; to learn to "read" the angles; to win tough rallies by hitting the right combination of shots; to start beating opponents who once beat them easily; and to keep raising their playing ability to a higher level. Mediocrity is nice when you're beginning, but who wants to be known around the club as a "veteran mediocre player"?

That's where this book comes in—to take you quickly from mediocrity so that you can play winning racquetball at every level you reach. I've organized my approach into a *center-court system* that focuses your overall strategy, your positioning, and your shot selection around that

The black paper on the court indicates the basic center-court area where the majority of balls will funnel during typical racquetball play. This is where the action is—and therefore where you want to try to play.

area of the court which receives most of the shots in a typical match.

Through detailed text and carefully staged photographs, I'll show you why the center-court approach offers you: (1) the fastest way to learn how to play the game right and (2) the soundest foundation there is for building a winning game—right through the professional ranks. I'll give you the basic strokes, the important shots, the match play tactics, and the mental techniques you need to help ensure successful center-court play.

On the serve, for example, you need to know the type of serves to hit and where to have the ball strike the front wall so that it angles into one of the back corners—away from center court. Special front-wall targets on page 139 will enable you to practice, and visualize, sound serves for when you go out to play.

Another crucial element in your success is your ability to sense ("read") where the ball will travel after caroming off various walls and the ceiling. Numerous photographs and diagrams should help you understand these spatial relationships if you haven't already tested them yourself out on the court. The angles and the trajectories in this game never change, so the faster you learn them, the quicker you will get into position to stroke the ball properly and the better accuracy you will have.

This book is also going to help you improve at the fastest possible rate by providing realistic practice drills for all of your important shots. Racquetball is beautifully designed for the player who wants to practice alone, or with a friend, since the front wall keeps the ball in play exactly as during a match. You can groove your strokes while evaluating their accuracy, and you can learn exactly what happens when the ball strikes the front wall from different locations on the court and at various heights.

This book is written for men, women, and juniors alike, without any differentiations made for basic techniques and strategies. That's the way I feel racquetball should be approached, as a game where everyone can build on the same fundamentals of good play. Women, for example, certainly don't need to learn their own special strokes or to adjust what I teach in these pages; with the right swing and a proper wrist snap at impact, they can hit the ball as hard as men.

I also want adults to realize that racquetball is an equally great sport for youngsters—one they can enjoy now and for the rest of their lives. Kids love the fact they can hit the ball as hard as they want, knowing they won't lose it, they won't break anybody's window, and they won't even necessarily lose the point. Meanwhile, they're developing their reflexes, learning what it means to be quick and resourceful, improving their hand-eye coordination, and building up their body's endurance.

When youngsters are starting out, try not to force technique on them. Expose them to proper strokes, the right serves, and center-court strategy—but then *let them play and have fun*. Their natural competitiveness will take over soon enough and they'll eventually want to learn to play the game correctly. Then the day will come when you'll be fighting for every point when they challenge you to a "friendly" match.

CHAPTER 1
AN OVERVIEW
OF THE GAME

By the latest estimate, there are over 2,000 racquetball facilities—and about 5,000,000 players—in the United States. If you live near any metropolitan area, or Odessa, Texas, or Waterville, Maine, or Boise, Idaho, you will have little difficulty finding a place to play. Indoor court facilities are springing up every day—some of them being financed by professional athletes from other sports who find that their investment also helps keep them in top shape during the off-season.

If there isn't a racquetball center in your town, search out any regulation handball court, since the dimensions and court markings are identical. Peggy Steding, one of the best women players in the game, is from Texas, where she learned how to play at the Odessa YMCA. The birthplace of higher-caliber racquetball in St. Louis was the Jewish Community Center. I started out playing at the Elks Club in St. Cloud, Minnesota.

You should also inquire at any college or university in your area, since many of them have racquetball courts. Your own kids may already be into racquetball at school, where the sport has become part of many physical education programs. The National Junior championships this past summer attracted over 200 players from 30 states.

You might even snoop around your local tennis club, since many established tennis centers, both public and private, have added racquetball courts.

EQUIPMENT

One appeal of racquetball is that "fashion" is unimportant; all you really need to wear is a pair of gym shorts, a T-shirt, socks, and tennis shoes, although sweatbands on the wrists and head are recommended if you perspire heavily. Many players also wear a glove to keep the racquet handle dry. Eye guards are also very appropriate.

Your one initial expense will be a racquet, which will range from $7 to about $50, already strung, and a can of balls for about $3. But you can rent various racquets at most clubs (50 cents to $1) while deciding which one is suited to your playing style.

Racquetball racquets are made of Fiber glass (left) and metal (middle) and are shorter and lighter than a tennis racquet (right). The racquetball ball is also smaller than the tennis ball.

The racquet is much shorter and lighter than a tennis racquet, and the smaller grip makes it feel more comfortable in your hand. Yet, choosing the correct racquet and the right-sized grip still involves some important questioning on your part.

My first racquet, purchased in 1971 back in St. Cloud, Minnesota, was a heavy old wood model that had a great big grip, because that's the kind of baseball bat handle size I had liked in college. I was a Nellie Fox-style hitter: using a thick handle, choking up, and making contact. But as I moved up in racquetball, I soon realized that I needed a much smaller racquet grip to allow my wrist to snap easily into the ball. A racquetball stroke is closer to Henry Aaron's wrist-snapping swing than Nellie Fox's punching style, and you might remember that Henry's bats all had very slim handles.

When you go to buy a racquet, make sure the grip is small enough to allow ample wrist action, yet not so small that the racquet turns in your hand. (A good test is to see that the middle and fourth finger meet the flesh of the thumb as you hold the racquet.) Grips range from extra small (3 5/16 inches) through small and medium to large, which is still only 4½ inches and which should be used only by those players with extremely long fingers. Many men imagine that their hands are bigger than they really are, and they like to buy the largest grip they can. A husky six-footer never believes me when I measure his hand and tell him he should have a "small" grip, but remember: you cannot snap your wrist properly if the grip is too large. I recently went from a medium (4 5/16 inches) to a small (4⅛ inches) to give me more wrist-snapping potential. Most men should use small or medium grips, and nearly all women will want to use an extra small or small.

There are a number of considerations used in selecting the racquet itself:

Length: About 18¼ inches is the best for most people, because it's the easiest to control, and control of the face of the racquet is what we all strive to attain. More length is an advantage for some people, but if you can't quickly control the racquet, then you pay too much of a penalty.

Weight: It's a matter of feel. You have to have enough racquet mass to project the ball off the strings, but not so much that it limits the amount of time you have to swing. A good compromise is about 270 or 275 grams.

Stiffness: Choosing between a stiff or flexible racquet is a matter of personal preference and playing style. Thus, I feel it's best to ask for demonstrator racquets at your club and test each type before you decide to buy.

Frame: Aluminum (or "metal") gives you an excellent combination of control and power if you keep the strings at a lower tension (*i.e.*, 25 pounds). This racquet also provides a good perimeter hit because of its durability around the outer edges. A fiber glass racquet has excellent touch and control. Its flexibility also helps absorb the shock when you hit the ball, making it easier on your arm.

Strings: Nylon strings are almost universally used in racquetball because they give good ball control, resist breakage, and hold tension effectively. Most racquets are factory-strung at between 22 and 30 pounds of tension.

Shape: It's a matter of personal preference whether the racquet frame is rectangular, teardrop, oval, or quadriform. The correlation between the shape of the head and its flexibility is so slight that it can only be noticed by a top-flight player.

There are a number of ways to keep your hand dry as you play, and thus ensure a firm grip. You can use a glove, a wristband, a towel, and a choice of racquet grips—rubber (left) or leather. Try the different combinations and find what works best for you.

Eye guards will enable you to play with greater safety—and confidence.

A CHECKLIST FOR OTHER EQUIPMENT

● All racquets must have a thong attached to the grip, which is wrapped around the player's wrist as a safety measure.

● A glove may be worn to help achieve a dry, sure grip, which is crucial to consistent shot-making. The glove should be lightweight, so as to minimize the loss of "feel," and it should be tacky. Some players, myself included, will use two or three gloves in the course of a hot match. I'd prefer not to lose this sensitivity, but I have no choice if I want to keep my racquet from turning or slipping in my hand.

● Nobody wears eye protectors, but everybody should. You may think it limits your vision a bit, but that is mostly psychological. They won't blind you nearly so badly as a sharply hit racquetball in the eye. Random mishaps can happen, especially among beginning players who don't always know when to duck.

● Whatever sneakers you choose to wear, make sure they are of high quality and a proper fit. It's also a good idea to wear two pairs of socks.

Friction will be absorbed between the socks and possibly spare you a few blisters.

● If you are playing on a budget, I recommend that you economize on everything but the racquet and the shoes. Play in old T-shirts and cutoffs if you must, but protect your feet and get a racquet that maximizes your ability.

LEARNING THE GAME

The cheapest and most direct way to get your first playing lesson is to collar an acquaintance—a spouse, friend, neighbor, business associate—who already knows how to play. That's where this book, even from one quick reading, should start paying dividends, by helping you understand the importance of what is being said as you get ready to play your first match.

From there, it's mainly a matter of practicing the rudimentary strokes, as they are applied to balls bouncing at various angles off the walls, the floor, and the ceiling. You want to strive for a "wristy" swing on the forehand—by snapping your wrist as much as possible when you contact the ball—and a good "shoulder" swing on the backhand, by getting the racquet pulled back so you don't punch at the ball. Work to bend the knees on both strokes so that you can contact the ball lower to the floor. The lower you can hit the ball into the front wall—with reasonable velocity—the more your opponent must hustle and stretch to keep the ball in play. Since the object is to kill the ball or hit the ball away from your opponent, your best shots will be: (1) the "kill," any ball that "rolls out" flat along the floor or takes two quick bounces before your opponent can reach it and (2) the "pass," a ball that first strikes the front wall and then travels either down the side wall or cross-court, thus forcing your opponent to move to one side of the court or the other.

If you want more formal instruction, and you don't mind spending a little money, you can find a qualified instructor at most centers or clubs in your area. You may even want to go off to a professional's week-long camp or clinic, just like your tennis friends. Dates and addresses normally are advertised in the racquetball magazines (*National Racquetball,* 4101 Dempster Street, Skokie, Illinois 60676, and *Racquetball,* 2670 Union Avenue, Suite 728, Memphis, Tennessee 38112.

Many touring professionals also give clinics in the cities where they stage their tournaments, from September through June. Free or inexpensive instruction may also be available through city recreation departments or university summer programs.

Once you feel your game is ready for organized competition, you'll

Down - the - wall passing shots on either side of the court will hit the front wall and force an opponent out of center court. Good passing shots will die in deep court and not come off the back wall.

Cross-court passing shots are aimed for the center of the front wall, about 3 feet high, so that they travel toward the back corner—and do not rebound off the back wall.

find that most local clubs have ladder competition (where members challenge one another for rankings within each ability division), while tournaments are always being organized to include novice, or "C," divisions everywhere. But please note: in most clubs, if you win a "C" division championship, you automatically move into the "B" division. So be prepared to improve your game accordingly.

ETIQUETTE AND SAFETY

Any time you put two people in a small room, playing a game where their goal is to control a certain area on the court while swinging at a ball with racquets, bruises and welts are going to occasionally result. The following guidelines should help you and your opponent avoid injuries, and also prevent disputes:

1. If you get hit by your opponent's racquet, it's *your* fault. You're obligated to give your opponent enough room to swing properly in close quarters, so if he or she has a long, wild follow - through (which is often true on the backhand), then keep your distance.

2. To avoid getting hit by the ball whenever your opponent is behind you, move far enough to one side to allow him a reasonable "hitting alley" to the front wall. If you stand in your opponent's hitting lane—whether he hits you with the ball or not—you're guilty of an "avoidable hinder." In tournament play, the referee has the right and should call an avoidable hinder as this play develops. This gives the point or the serve to your opponent.

2

3. Another avoidable hinder occurs when you fail to move out of the way of your opponent so that he can move in to take a proper swing.

3

There's a mutual respect required in playing this game properly to keep it from sliding into guerrilla warfare. Give your opponents what they are due, and let them have the freedom to swing freely, without having to worry about hitting you with the ball, or the racquet. To play otherwise is to ruin the spirit of a great game.

CHAPTER 2

THE CENTER-COURT STRATEGY

To win consistently in racquetball, you must maintain a good center-court position as much as possible throughout the match. This area—which extends from just behind the back service line to about 9 feet from the back wall and to within 2 or 3 feet of both side walls—has always influenced good racquetball. Yet many players fail to realize that for experts, intermediates, and novices alike, *whoever controls center court controls the rally*. You may not win the rally when you out-position your opponent—good strokes and proper execution are equally important—but the percentages will always be in your favor.

There are two basic reasons why the center-court strategy encompasses *every* player in the game. First, simple geometry dictates that any ball hit with reasonable velocity that strikes a side wall—either on its way to, or returning from, the front wall—will angle toward the middle of the court. Only a perfect or nearly perfect shot will go for an irretrievable "kill" in the front court, or an unreachable "pass" in the back court, against a well-positioned opponent. And, secondly, *perfection is a low-percentage proposition*. We either hit the ball too high on the front wall, or we catch a side wall. Even at the professional level, most matches are played with both players continually jockeying for position in center court, because that's where the ball keeps coming. The speed of the ball allows minimal time to swing properly, and even the slightest error will angle the ball toward the middle.

Therefore, by learning to operate inside the center-court area, you're always going to be close to the heart of the action—just one or two steps and a good stretch away from virtually every ball your opponent hits that isn't killed in the front court. You greatly reduce wasted energy chasing down balls, and you give yourself the best chance to play the game offensively—the way it is intended.

Beginners, don't get scared off. The center-court strategy is easily understood and it will enable you to walk out on the court with the confidence that you already know where to position yourself—no matter how many walls the ball might carom off—and where you want to try to aim your own shots. Racquetball is a fast-moving, rapid-fire, quick-reacting type of game that can thoroughly confuse the inexperienced player. It's hard to keep your bearings in the heat of play as the ball ricochets about the court while you try to anticipate where it's going to end up and what shot you should hit. But a knowledge of center-court strategy gives you an anchoring point around which the entire game swirls; it enables you to see the forest *and* the trees.

LOCATING YOUR CENTER-COURT "X"

The center-court area always remains the same size, but your ideal coverage position within this area will shift in relation to the ball, your opponent's position, and the accuracy of his or her shots. Thus, your imaginary center-court "X" will normally be located about 3 to 5 feet behind the back service line and about midway between the side walls, slightly to the side to which you have hit the ball. *Ideally, this will leave you equidistant from the crucial court zones that you must cover.*

In good racquetball, "floating" your center-court "X" to your opponent's side of the court will enable you to anticipate his kill attempt into the nearest front corner, or his passing shot down that side wall—his quickest and best scoring opportunities. If he tries to go cross-court, the ball has to travel a longer distance and you gain an extra split-second to cover the shot.

Conversely, if your opponent is unable to kill the ball into the front corners or drive it along the side wall, then you can move your "X" into the middle, and even toward the opposite side of the court, since most of his cross-court shots are going to wind up there.

When you play a person whose game emphasizes successful kill attempts into the front wall, then you'll want to shift your "X" forward 2 or 3 feet to give yourself a better chance to dig up as many of these shots as possible. Or, if your opponent likes to hit cross-court passes with a lot of velocity, your "X" will probably float back 2 or 3 feet from its normal location, toward the side of the court the ball is coming to.

Most C, and even some B, players will find that this deeper position—
about 27 to 29 feet from the front wall—can actually be effective against
hard-hitting opponents who are unable to keep the ball low on the front
wall, and whose shots thus always take their second bounce in the deep
back court, or even rebound hard off the back wall.

When your opponent has the ability to kill the ball into the front corner, or to
hit down-the-wall passing shots, you must position yourself on that side of
the court from which he or she is hitting.

When play shifts to the left side of the court, shift your position accordingly, as the player in front is doing here. She anticipates the ball going into the left corner, or along the left wall, but she is ready to turn and cover her opponent's cross-court pass.

JOCKEYING FOR CENTER-COURT POSITION

You may be thinking: "If the center court is so crucial, why don't people just head for their 'X' after every shot and wait for the ball to come to them?"

Theoretically, that's what you want to do; you always want to be focused on the middle of center court. But keep in mind one basic fact: *nobody owns center court.* It's always up for grabs, depending upon who has the best anticipation and the quickest, most accurate strokes. Both players have the right to use that area, but only when they are entitled to it.

The rule of thumb is: When you hit the ball down the sides of the court, you can remain in center court or move into that area as your opponent

These players are jockeying for position in center court. They both are in good coverage and scoring positions, and the rally will probably be determined by who has the most efficient stroke in this area.

retrieves your shot. But whenever you bring the ball into the middle, you're obligated to move far enough to one side to allow your opponent sufficient room to swing properly and to have an open hitting lane to the front wall. This doesn't mean you have to vacate center court completely; you may only have to move 2 or 3 feet away, to the perimeter. Then, once your opponent has hit, move right back toward the middle, unless his shot forces you elsewhere.

In good racquetball, control of center court is rarely clear-cut. Both players are in that area most of the match, 3 to 5 feet apart, jockeying for the *better* position—not so much in a physical, elbowing sense, but with the shots they hit. This puts the emphasis on key fundamentals that are applicable to players at every ability level as they maneuver for consistent center-court positioning:

• Whenever possible, strive for kill shots into the front corners or straight into the front wall, or passing shots that drive your opponent to the perimeter of center court. Even if your opponent retrieves your passing shot, you now control the middle and he must try to drive you out with a difficult shot.

• Hit your passing shots low enough on the front wall (under 3 feet, assuming reasonable velocity) to keep them from rebounding off the back wall and giving your opponent an easier shot.

• If you're unsure of what to do, always aim to hit the front wall *first* — as low and as hard as possible — and you will keep good pressure on your opponent. Even if the ball heads straight for your opponent in center court, the velocity will force him to execute a quick "reflex" stroke, and it may even handcuff him enough to force an outright error.

• Hold your position in center court by volleying every ball that comes to you in the air at *about waist level or below*. If you let these shots go by you, thinking you'll have an easier play when the ball rebounds off the back wall, then you're opting for defensive — and ultimately losing — racquetball. A smart opponent will simply take over center-court control as you move back into the deep court area, and he'll be waiting for you to hit anything but a perfect shot off the back wall. (As I'll discuss later, when the ball is coming to you in the air above chest level, let it go by and it will rebound off the back wall into center court for an easy "plum shot.")

• Learn to think aggressively — and offensively. You're always looking for scoring opportunities, and when you get them, take them; don't hesitate and simply try to keep the ball in play. The average rally is not very long, and if you pass up an offensive opportunity, your opponent may end the rally before you get another chance. The style of play I advocate might seem, and look, a little wild and frenzied, but that's the way racquetball is. So get yourself to think: "This *is* the way to play. I want to be obsessed by the center court."

The player on the left is in center court, but well away from where he should be positioned, as indicated by the white "X." He leaves his opponent a wide-open court on the right side.

The player here has positioned himself too far forward during the rally—in the middle of the service zone—and thus leaves himself vulnerable to cross-court passes.

When you position yourself too deep on the court, you have a difficult time retrieving your opponent's kill attempts.

GROOVING YOUR CENTER-COURT POSITION

You want to visualize the heart of center court as your home base, a place where you feel comfortable, even if you have to share the area with your opponent. Following are some ways you can incorporate the center-court position into your playing style so that it becomes instinctive:

1. Think of a magnet in the middle of center court that is always drawing you—as well as the ball—into that area. After virtually every shot you take, try to funnel toward the magnet and as close to your ideal position as possible. If your opponent is already there, then move in alongside as close as etiquette and good sense allow.

2. Find a friend who will play a match with an "X" taped directly in the middle of center court. This will give you a specific visual reference—out of the corner of your eye—as you move about the court. You should also check yourself as you play and see how close you're positioning yourself to that "X."

3. Play several matches where you tell yourself: "I'm going to learn what it really means to play center court. I'm going to stand right in the middle of this area without my opponent and force him to hit the ball away from me. I'll sacrifice some shots into the corners and down the side walls, but I'll take advantage of the percentages, since most balls are going to come to me in the middle." This kind of extreme positioning may feel awkward and unnatural at first, especially if you're changing some ingrained coverage habits. But you're going to start winning more matches this way, and that should loosen you up nicely.

CHAPTER 3
COVERING THE COURT

Properly played, racquetball is a game where you are bending and stretching and continuously moving from shot to shot, with few delays and breaks in the action. Thus, if you hope to play your best for the entire match, your goal must be to *conserve energy while reaching as many balls as possible*.

For example, the court will seem much larger than it really is when you're always out of position. Smart opponents will have more room to hit the ball *away* from you, and though you might have excellent retrieving ability, your body won't last long as you charge pell-mell after every ball. In the end, you will lose to better players because of one basic fact: you are running *away from the game*.

But when you focus all of your movements around your center-court position, *the game comes to you*. Nearly all of your work will be confined to a coverage area that stretches only about 11 to 15 feet behind the back service line and to within about 2 feet of the side walls. Your speed, size, and stretching ability will determine how effectively and efficiently you cover this center-court area, but if you play it right, you will be in a better position to retrieve rally shots into the back 7 or 8 feet of the court, and anticipation will usually enable you to cut off passing shots within 2 or 3 feet of the side wall. The only time you will venture into the front-court area will be to dig up your opponent's kill attempts or a weak shot that has barely reached the front wall.

The hitter shows how an easy and comfortable stretch will enable her to cover nearly all of the center-court area from the "X." With a forceful stretch, she could come within a foot of the side walls.

1

2

The following three points should help you expand your *offensive hitting range* within the center-court area by eliminating much of the guesswork and hesitation you might have in playing the ball and by making you more aggressive as you cover the court.

1. Learning to "Read" the Front Wall

Here are some hints for judging more precisely where the ball will travel after rebounding *straight off the front wall,* without hitting a side wall—and what you should do, assuming you have a good center-court position:

• If your opponent's shot is traveling at a reasonable velocity and strikes the front wall 0 to 12 inches off the floor, its bounce will pull you into the front court, and will very likely result in a kill.

• A ball hitting 12 to 24 inches high with good speed will bounce once and carry into or near the center-court area, where you must cut it off before it gets past you, because it will die in deep court. You may think you have to move up into the service zone area in order to protect yourself against these low drives by your opponent, *but this is a common myth.* Even a ball that hits only 18 inches high on the front wall, with good velocity, will still take its second bounce well beyond the back service line. Furthermore, when you try to position yourself in front of the center-court area, you leave yourself extremely vulnerable to passing shots.

• If the ball hits about 36 inches high, then it will come back to you in the air at about knee to waist level, and you will want to volley it—at whatever level it is coming. Don't back up and try to let it drop lower, and don't let it go to the back wall, because your goal is to maintain center-court positioning.

• Any ball that strikes the front wall about 48 inches up should be a welcome sight: let it go by, because it will either hit the back wall on one bounce or in the air, and then rebound into center court for an easy setup.

Although plain old experience will teach you where the ball actually travels straight off the front wall, you'll make some interesting discoveries for yourself by practicing on an empty court and by watching other people play.

For example, put a piece of tape at one-foot intervals up the front wall so you have an accurate visual reference, and then stand about 30 feet away and blast forehands toward the tape. See for yourself where the ball actually takes its first bounce, and how far it carries toward the back wall when it strikes the front wall at various heights and speeds. Chances are you'll discover that the ball bounces much deeper on the court than you might have thought.

Let's say you're in center court, 25 feet from the front wall, and the ball hits 18 inches high with good velocity. The crucial thing to remember is that you will never have to thrust forward to reach this shot before it bounces twice. Just stand there at 25 feet, with your weight evenly distributed, and let the ball come to you easily on one bounce. You might have to stretch and get low as you stroke the ball, but you'll never have to hurry forward and then lunge to make your hit.

By experimenting in this way, you not only improve your shot-making skills, but you sharpen your perception of what it means to keep the ball low off the front wall — and the setups you give your opponent when you leave it up high. You also gain a much better sense of where similar shots by your opponent are going to land.

You can also learn a lot by watching other players as you wait for a

court or as you cool down following a match. When you're not playing, you'll find it's much easier to notice patterns occurring and see where the ball goes after hitting at different speeds, angles, and heights off the front wall, and how it then reacts off the side walls and the back wall.

Also try to observe passing shot angles. It's easy to be fooled by the geometry involved, unless you're an experienced pool player. I know that when I place beginners in the middle of the court and tell them, "Hit the ball down the side wall into the back corner, but don't hit the side wall," their first couple of tries invariably strike too close to that side wall—instead of hitting virtually in the middle of the front wall. Thus, the ball proceeds to ricochet off the side wall and into mid-court.

The player on the left is turned slightly so that he can study his opponent as she hits the ball. His knees are bent, his racquet is carried in a relaxed ready position between his knees and thighs, and he's ready to quickly prepare for his next shot.

2.Anticipation

Good anticipation is a mental skill that will improve your playing ability and help you neutralize a stronger opponent, even as you are working to develop better strokes. Racquetball is like a fast-moving chess game, and your ability to anticipate your opponent's shots can gain you that extra split-second that allows you to reach more balls, or to set up better for your shots.

Your anticipation should start as soon as you see your opponent start to set up on his shot. If he is hitting from off to one side, turn slightly so you can watch the ball come into his racquet. Then study his body positioning and his swing, and try to anticipate either a defensive shot like the ceiling ball (the racquet will be traveling on an upward angle, since this shot must hit the ceiling before rebounding into the back-court area), or an offensive shot like the kill or pass, where the racquet angles downward from its ready position around the head. Most beginning and intermediate players practically call out their shots by making no attempt to disguise their stroke—and they usually get away with it because their opponent isn't watching for clues.

You may not be able to determine exactly *where* your opponent is going to hit the ball, but you can anticipate when he's going to hit so you can ready yourself for probable center-court action. Expect errors. Don't be surprised if your opponent hits a ball that you can't reach. Remember, you can cover nearly the entire court by being in center court.

Too many people walk onto the court prepared to play defensively, and when the match begins you can see them thinking: "Opponent, please don't hit a winner." They don't realize that errors are much more frequent. By waylaying these shots into the middle, and returning them offensively whenever possible, you will stretch your opponent from one side of the court to the other. This will give him less time to set up and swing properly, which should lead to even more errors. So you will get a nice cycle going.

3. Moving to the Ball

Racquetball is such a fast-moving, quick-starting sport that good strokes will be wasted if you don't have the footwork and reactions to reach as many balls as possible with enough time to set up properly. To help you move to the ball better—keeping in mind that you rarely will take more than two or three steps from a good center-court position—try to learn the following basics:

● Start preparing for your next shot as soon as you complete your follow-through. Relocate your center-court "X" in relation to where the ball is traveling, and where your opponent is located.

• Trust your instincts as soon as the ball leaves your opponent's racquet—if not sooner. In fast-paced racquetball, you'll seldom have time to confirm the exact direction of every shot. If you see the ball deflect off any side wall, hold your ground near the middle because the ball will rebound into that area.

• If you're playing center court, this is a game of hitting a ball that's coming fairly close to your body, or taking one long step or a long stretch to reach a ball that's traveling along a side wall. It's not a game of pitter-patter little steps, or a long series of steps. If the ball is hit very low on the front wall, then you'll have to move forward, but you're only going to have time to take one or two thrusting steps before the ball bounces twice.

• As you wait to see the direction of your opponent's shot, keep your heels on the ground, with your weight evenly distributed. You don't want to be up on your toes, as in tennis, because most balls are going to come to you with good velocity in the center-court area and you'll want to be in a solid position to hit. As the caliber of your competition improves, you'll probably have to be a little more cautious of your opponent's kill attempts and be ready to move forward more often.

• When waiting for the ball, plant your feet about 2 feet apart—wide enough to give you a strong foundation, yet close enough to enable you to really stretch out or move toward the ball. Try to work out a comfortable compromise.

• Keep your knees slightly bent as you move about the court, with your back relatively straight or at just a slight angle. Not only will you play better, but you'll *look* like a racquetball player. You want to move toward offensive shots in a low neutral position because the ball is coming low and your goal is to return it as low as possible into the front wall. Thus, you're already down close to the floor for the shot before you even start your swing, and you'll always have good balance—ready to thrust out quickly for the ball, wherever it goes. But when you remain in a high position by failing to bend your legs, you have to go down to hit the ball properly, then you come back up, and then you go down again for the next shot. If the ball goes quickly to one side and you're up high in a stiff-legged position, you have a harder time pushing off with your back leg and stretching out toward the ball. You also won't have good balance.

• As you move about the court, carry your racquet comfortably around waist level so you can bring it up quickly into a ready position. You'll lose too much time if you carry it down around your ankles.

Knowing how to dive properly for the ball will stretch your court coverage ability. Notice that the hitter's body is in control and that her left arm provides support. She knows she must snap her wrist at impact to generate sufficient velocity on the ball.

CHAPTER 4

THE FOREHAND

Good court coverage can take you a long way in this game—but only if you have sound, fundamental strokes that produce the accurate shots you need to gain and maintain center-court positioning.

I'll start with the forehand, since it's the single most important stroke in the game. Not only can you play about two-thirds of the court with the forehand, but this is also the same basic stroke you use for your most common serves, the low drive and the "Z." The forehand is such a "confidence" stroke for nearly all players that many professionals even run around their strong backhand in order to hit a forehand just 3 or 4 feet from the left wall.

The wrist snap is the single most crucial element in grooving a forehand that delivers both power and accuracy. In fact, the only way to generate any real velocity on your shots is to *snap your wrist forcibly into the ball at impact*. As strong as you may be, if you try to play with a fixed-wrist swing, like in tennis, you'll end up punching the ball weakly to the front wall. This may give you good control, but your shots will lack the sting to make you a threat against better players.

THE GRIP

The racquetball racquet is so much shorter and lighter than a tennis racquet that you may feel the grip you use is unimportant. But if you don't have a proper grip, you will have to make subtle adjustments in your swing in order to have the racquet face vertical at impact. These "adjustments" lead to inconsistent shots.

Like most instructors, I advocate "shaking hands" with the racquet handle as you grasp hold, so that the "V" formed by the thumb and index finger is directly on top of the racquet handle. The racquet is small, but don't hold it like a club; have the index finger slightly extended. Maintain a fairly relaxed grip until just before impact, then tighten the fingers to ensure a solid hit. Holding a constant death grip on the racquet throughout every swing will lead to extreme fatigue in your forearm muscles and the chance of a strained hitting arm.

1

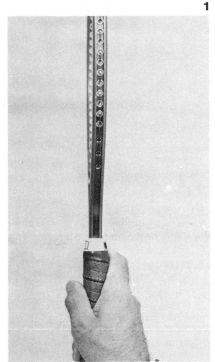

THE FOREHAND GRIP

This shows the proper grip, with the "V" formed by your thumb and index finger comfortably on top of the racquet handle.

2

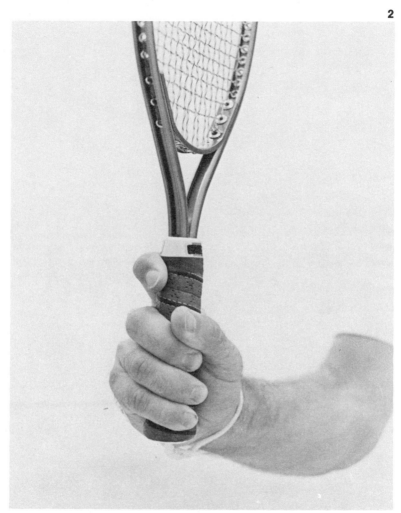

This is the grip as seen from below, with the thumb resting against the middle finger, and the index finger slightly extended

3

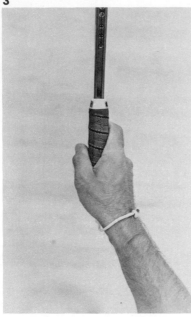

The grip is held too deep in the palm and too far down on the racquet. You lose some control of the face of the racquet.

4

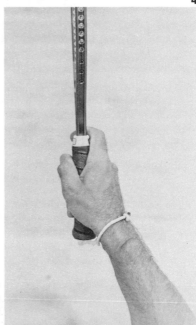

The grip is held too high on the racquet. Choking up like this minimizes the amount of power that you can generate with the racquet.

AN OVERVIEW OF THE IDEAL SWING

Ideally, you want to reach the ball in time to set up properly and stride into the ball with a full-body swing. Because this is the stroke you want to build your game around, I'll discuss it first in this chapter. But, eventually, as you try to maintain center-court positioning, the pace of the game will often force you to hit from an open stance with a shortened, but still forceful, swing. This "reflex" stroke is equally important in good racquetball and will be described later in the chapter.

First, let's assume that your opponent's shot is going to allow you to take a full swing. When you reach your hitting location (with your racquet at about chest level), quickly put your racquet up into a set position at around head height, or slightly above, with the wrist cocked. Have your body turned so that your non-hitting shoulder is facing the front wall.

You must rely on experience to help you sense *when* to actually stride into the ball and *when* to start the downward motion of your hitting shoulder and racquet arm. But don't let these movements occur simultaneously or you will lose considerable power. You first want to step out about 12 to 20 inches and transfer your weight to this front leg. Leave your racquet up in its cocked position, for it must come through *last* in your stroking sequence.

Have your hitting shoulder and arm actually start down as you drive forward with your front thigh and uncoil with both hips into the ball. Bend your back knee and drop your hitting shoulder so that you can tuck the elbow in close to the body. Then pull through with your forearm while the wrist remains laid back, the racquet basically pointing to the back wall.

Just before impact off the front foot, *snap that wrist forward,* and the racquet will come ripping through to make contact. Let your wrist snap through completely and have the racquet remain at about waist level until safely after impact. Remember, you want the ball to travel into the front wall on the same height, or lower, than it arrived, and this requires a flat, or level, follow-through. The racquet will then come up naturally by your left ear.

Strive to maintain good body balance at the completion of your stroke so that you are ready to break in any direction for your opponent's next shot. Ideally, you want to have a nice flowing motion from stroke to stroke.

THE FULL-BODY FOREHAND SWING

1

The hitter has his racquet pulled back with his wrist fully cocked. His left arm is comfortably in front of his body, his knees are slightly bent, and his back is fairly straight.

The hitter strides into the ball, then dips his hitting shoulder slightly to help lower the racquet. The right knee is starting to bend extensively and the left arm is starting to pull the body through the swing.

The racquet is laid back and the wrist is still fully cocked just before contact. The right arm is bent at the elbow and tucked close to the right side of the body, while the legs are generating power.

Contact is made off the front foot, with the racquet face vertical at impact and traveling on a straight line into the ball. Notice the extensive bending of the legs, and how the player's eyes are focused on the point of impact.

The wrist has snapped through the ball and the left arm has been thrown out of the way to give the racquet full clearance on the follow-through. The body stays low and the legs remain bent until the swing has been completed.

6

The racquet is pulled up behind the left side of the head on the follow-through, and the wrist has been fully snapped. Notice that the body has retained good balance throughout the swing.

Seen from behind, notice how the right arm should be bent at the elbow as you drive into the ball, and how the elbow is tucked in close to the body. This enables the racquet to remain cocked until the last instant before impact, and you can approach the ball on a low, flat plane.

IMPORTANT ELEMENTS OF THE SWING

Following is a more detailed look at key elements in your forehand swing. You might find it helpful to take out your racquet, get in front of a mirror, and go through the motions I'm describing. Check your body positions at different stages of the swing and start working on these correct "feelings" now—before you even go back to the court.

Lower Body Movements

By failing to use your lower body properly—the hips, the knees, and the thighs—you create two problems for yourself. First, you place excess pressure on your hitting shoulder and arm to produce the velocity you want on your shots. This strain can result in a sore shoulder and/or a sore elbow. Second, you have less consistency in driving the ball low into the front wall.

Here, then, are some thoughts about your lower body movements:

• When you can take a good, healthy stride into the ball, you form a solid base of support on the front leg. And by thrusting off this thigh as you stroke the ball, you generate considerable power.

• As the front thigh pushes forward, the back knee should start to bend. This helps lower your upper body so that the racquet can come through the ball on as flat an angle, or plane, as possible.

• Meanwhile, your hips should be pivoting around to deliver their power. For imagery purposes, you're actually driving your right buttock into the shot.

Getting Low to the Ball

To play this game right, you want to drive the ball as low and on as straight a line as possible into the front wall. This means you must lower your hitting arm in such a way that the racquet can drive through the ball flat, on the same level as your wrist or slightly lower.

Moving to the ball with your legs already comfortably bent, and then staying low with the body, is the most efficient way of setting up for low-drive and kill-shot attempts. But most people find it too difficult to use their knees this much; play is so continuous that it takes strong, youthful legs and good agility to keep scurrying about the court in a low position.

Fortunately, however, you can compensate on most balls by mastering your upper body movements and bending at the waist. If you drop your hitting shoulder as you start your swing, and tuck your elbow in about 4 or

HIP ROTATION ON THE FOREHAND

This sequence shows the powerful rotation of the hips that you seek on your forehand swing. Notice in the final two pictures how the left hip "opens up" while the right hip thrusts powerfully into the ball.

1

5 inches from your side, you enable the racquet to come through low and flat. It has a nice range over which to contact the ball and drive it low into the front wall.

However, if you try to play with stiff legs and no bending at the waist, you must swing down at the ball on such an angle that you have only a tiny area in which to contact the ball properly. If your timing is slightly off, the ball will either go into the floor for a "skip" or high into the front wall.

The Non-Hitting Arm

Most people don't know what to do with their left arm. Through instinct or from their own experience in tennis, it often gets in the way and can limit the freedom of their swing. The problem often starts with the left hand. If you're in the habit of touching this hand to your racquet handle as you take the racquet up into its set position, that's like touching home plate every time. It keeps you from pulling the racquet up as quickly as you want, and as far back as you should. You'll end up punching at the ball rather than taking a full-body swing.

By keeping your left hand off the racquet, you make it easier to keep the arm itself from getting too close to the body. Study the pictures here to notice how the arm should be pulled back out of the way as you take your swing. Then make sure you consciously check yourself during a match and as you practice.

The Racquet Arm and Wrist

In tennis, you might pay $20 an hour to a pro who tells you repeatedly, "Hit with a fixed wrist." That kind of advice is deadly in racquetball. You want to use all the wrist action you can get on your basic forehand stroke; when you take an imaginary swing, there should be a whooshing sound by the racquet strings in the impact area.

Stand in front of a mirror for three other crucial checkpoints: (1) Is the wrist cocked as you hold it in a set position behind your head? (2) Is it still laid back and cocked just before impact and ready to deliver an explosive snap? (3) Is the elbow bent and tucked in close enough to your body so that the forearm, the bicep, and the shoulder can all uncoil at the ball?

If your hitting arm is as straight as a tennis swing, it will prevent you from snapping the wrist properly. You must bend the elbow, and have the wrist cocked back as you come into the ball. Then snap that wrist forward at impact.

Contacting the Ball

If you have time, and you can still maintain a good center-court position, let the ball drop as low as you can before you hit it. The closer the ball is to the floor when you make contact, the easier it is to keep it low on the front wall-providing, of course, you swing properly. But always remember, if you're going to play center-court racquetball, *you must learn to hit the ball at the height it comes to you, waist high or below.* Except on obvious "plum" balls, you won't have the luxury to maneuver yourself so that the ball always bounces nice and low around calf level. If you try to play this way, then you're letting the ball play you.

Meanwhile, try to watch the ball make contact with the strings. This kind of focusing helps keep your head down through impact, and thus ensures a more solid hit and better accuracy. When you get too eager to see where the ball is going, you tend to lift your head up at impact, which in turn pulls your racquet up too soon.

The Follow-Through

Not only do you want to get down to the ball at contact, but you want to stay down until your stroke is completed. Don't abruptly pull up, worrying about your opponent's shot. Tell yourself, "Hit and stay down," so that you drive the ball low with a follow-through that is complete and forceful.

WRIST ACTION ON THE FOREHAND

In this sequence: (1) the racquet is laid back and the wrist is fully cocked; (2) the wrist is starting to extend and the racquet is coming into the ball; (3) contact is made off the front foot; (4) the wrist is still breaking as the racquet has snapped through the ball; (5) the wrist has snapped fully.

1

2

3

4

5

THE OPEN-STANCE SWING

When you get into close-quarters rallies with your opponent, 20 to 27 feet from the front wall, the ball will come too fast for you to set up properly and take a full-body swing. To hold your own, and to win matches, you need to know how to swing effectively from an open stance (where you are facing the front wall or slightly toward the side wall with both feet pointed in the same direction). Your stroke will have a shorter backswing and follow-through than your regular swing, and you won't be able to step into the ball; otherwise the basics are quite similar.

Here are the key elements to keep in mind:

• In good racquetball, a lot of action is going to occur in the front part of center court, and the winner is going to be the one who has the best reactions and the most efficient shortened stroke.

• Direction is the key, since all the power you need is being supplied by your opponent's shot—providing you make solid contact. If you stroke the ball properly this close to the front wall, it will go for a kill, or zip by your opponent for a passing shot winner.

• Hitting from an open stance limits your leg power, but you can compensate and still generate good power by using the proper wrist-snapping motion, shoulder power, and slight hip rotation. This velocity on the ball is crucial for when you are forced to use the open swing from farther back in center court, such as when you play a hard-hitter who keeps pounding that ball straight into the front wall.

• When you're flailing away near the front court, you'll establish a better base of support by planting your feet wider than shoulder-width apart. With a little knee bend, you can stretch out for the ball in either direction and maintain good balance. Conversely, if you're waiting for the ball in a high position with your feet close together, you'll lack the power to thrust out quickly for a ball that's going by you. And you'll tend to lose your balance when you do.

• Not only is it more effective to have a shortened swing when you're maneuvering for position in center court, it's a common courtesy. You and your opponent should be able to hit your shots freely and reposition properly in close quarters without the fear of getting hit in the face with the racquet.

THE OPEN-STANCE SWING

This is the short, powerful stroke you need when the action is fast and furious and you don't have time to step into the ball and take a full-body swing. Notice in this sequence how the hitter has his feet wide apart and pointed in the same direction, toward the right front corner. This enables him to pull through quickly with his hips and his left arm.

The racquet is not taken back as high as in a regular swing, and the follow-through is shortened. Otherwise, everything else is similar: the racquet is cocked in its set position near the head; the left arm is thrown out of the way to give the racquet complete clearance; the hitting arm makes the same tucking motion; the knees are bent through the swing (though not as severely); the head remains down until the follow-through is completed.

1

4

PRACTICING THE FOREHAND

One of the nice things about racquetball is that you can improve your skills noticeably, all by yourself on an empty court. The following two practice drills can help you groove a reliable forehand stroke:

1. Stand at various distances from the front wall, drop the ball and let it bounce once, and then practice hitting kill shots, down-the-wall passing shots, cross-court passes, and front-wall pinches, shots that strike the front wall and one side wall, in either sequence, as low and tight in the corner as possible. Place tape 3 feet high on the front wall and strive to hit every shot between the tape and the floor—but keep moving the tape down as you improve.

2. Hit the ball off the front wall so that it comes to you in center court on one easy bounce. Then get your racquet set, step into the ball, and go for a front-wall winner. Keep repeating this sequence so that you can work on your timing and a smooth stroke. Then you might want to go a step further by trying to re-drive or re-kill the kill attempts you leave too high. This is excellent practice for your open-stance "reflex" shot up near the front court. It sharpens your reaction time, helps you develop quick racquet action, and forces you to follow through on balance so you're ready for the next shot.

You may think you need to know a lot more "sophisticated" drills on the forehand, but these two drills will enable you to practice every forehand you could realistically want to use during a match.

FOUR COMMON ERRORS

1

The left hand is on the racquet just before the racquet is pulled back. This keeps you from getting your racquet back quick enough or far enough.

2

The left arm is too close into the body, and this will constrict the freedom of your swing.

3

Here there is a lack of knee bend during the swing and an improper follow-through, with the racquet pointed toward the floor.

4

The racquet arm is much too straight, and this robs you of the forceful power of the tucking motion.

A FOREHAND CHECKLIST

1. Have your body in a good ready position: feet about shoulder-width apart; back fairly straight; legs comfortably bent so they can be used in the total body swing.

2. Have the racquet set quickly and wrist cocked.

3. Take a good stride into the ball.

4. Drive forward with your front thigh into the ball as you dip your hitting shoulder.

5. Rotate your hips into the ball.

6. Throw your left arm out of the way so it doesn't limit your swing.

7. Bend your back knee to get low. This will help to get your racquet on a lower plane.

8. Keep a strong, tucking motion with your hitting arm bent at the elbow and tucked in close to the right side of your body as you come into the ball.

9. Have your wrist laid back and cocked until just before impact.

10. Snap your wrist forcibly at impact; don't punch at the ball.

11. Contact the ball with a racquet face that is vertical at impact and traveling on a horizontal plane.

12. Keep your eyes on the ball and stay down with your body.

13. Complete your swing with a natural follow-through.

CHAPTER 5

THE BACKHAND

I know players in clubs across the country to whom racquetball is an obsession. They're good athletes, they're strong, they crack a good forehand, they have good serves, and they know all the fundamental shots. But they have one fatal weakness that overrides all their strengths: *they can't hit a backhand.* Oh, they usually manage to keep the ball in play with a short little punch stroke, but ultimately—no matter how much they hustle and scrap for every point—they lose to the better all-around players because: (1) they hit too many backhand "plums" to their opponent, and (2) they are unable to maintain consistent center-court positioning.

Mastering an accurate backhand that has both power and direction is no easy task, as we all eventually learn. For one thing, it's simply not as natural to hit as the forehand. We grow up playing sports off our dominant side—hitting a baseball, driving a golf ball, throwing a football—and it's an uncomfortable feeling to turn your body around and try to hit a coordinated backhand. Second, if you can do nothing else on the forehand but snap your wrist at impact, you'll still hit the ball hard. This wrist action is usually a little more difficult to learn on the backhand, and relatively ineffective if you fail to rotate your hitting shoulder and hips into the ball.

These initial experiences on the backhand are what lead many people to instinctively shorten their swing so they can at least punch or flick the ball back safely to the front wall. But this is to resign themselves to defensive racquetball, and my feeling is that everybody should be able to play the game somewhat offensively. The backhand certainly doesn't have to be a weak link in *your* game—providing you develop a confident approach and apply several fundamentals that lead to a full-body stroke.

THE GRIP

Whenever time permits, I like people to switch grips from the forehand to the backhand by moving their hand slightly to the left on the racquet handle. This facilitates a more natural swing.

With a little practice, you'll find you can easily switch grips as you move toward the ball. Keep your racquet hand relaxed and let your fingers and hand do the work. It may be tempting to hold the throat of the racquet with your non-hitting hand as you switch, but this will usually lead to a slow and constricted backswing.

When playing close to the front court, if you don't have time—or the quick hand movement—to switch, then maintain your forehand grip and go for a direction shot into the left corner or down the left wall. If you try to hold one grip for all of your strokes (slightly between the conventional grips), you will be forced to make slight adjustments in your basic swing in order to produce a vertical racquet face at impact.

THE BACKHAND GRIP

Your grip is the same as on the forehand, except that the "V" formed by your thumb and index finger moves slightly to the left and is directly on top of the left diagonal on your racquet handle.

AN OVERVIEW OF THE FULL-BODY SWING

When starting out with this stroke, keep in mind that most people have weak backhands because they fail to take a healthy swing at the ball— even when they have time to set up properly. So as you work on the techniques in this chapter, strive at first for velocity and don't worry about where the ball goes. The key thing to learn is how *good* it feels to rip that ball into the front wall; this gives you the confidence to never settle for a safe little punch shot.

Just as on the forehand, bring your racquet up to about chest level as you move into position for your shot, and then quickly pull it back behind your head as you set up. Your body will be facing the side wall as the ball is nearing your hitting area.

When the ball enters your hitting zone, rotate your upper body back toward the back wall so that your hitting shoulder is actually facing that wall. Try to feel those back muscles stretch out as you coil.

Now step diagonally toward the ball and transfer your weight out onto the front thigh. Thrust off this thigh as your hips and hitting shoulder start to rotate into the shot, but remember: keep the racquet pulled back so that it comes through last in the stroking sequence.

As the ball approaches your front foot, you want to be coming through with your entire arm and then the cocked wrist, which snaps through the ball at the last instant. But *hold the wrist solid after it has snapped and you have made contact* —don't let it roll over. Instead, pull through with your arm and shoulder. Your follow-through should carry around horizontally, at about waist level, so that you drive the ball back at the same height, or lower, than it arrived (assuming, of course, that your racquet face was vertical at impact).

THE FULL-BODY BACKHAND STROKE

1

In setting up for the swing: the racquet is pulled back; the wrist is fully cocked; the hitting arm is bent; the knees are comfortably bent; the shoulders are coiled and pointing toward the back wall.

2

The hitter is getting a forceful thrust off the front leg (with his weight heavily on that leg), and the hitting arm is starting to extend—but the racquet is still kept back, with the wrist cocked.

3

Just before contact, the right arm is nearly extended, the wrist is starting to break, and the shoulder is pulling the racquet through the shot.

4

Contact is made off the front foot. The racquet arm is extended, the wrist has completed its snapping process, and the eyes are focused down at the point of impact.

5

In the beginning of the follow-through, the wrist has been fully snapped and is being held firm. Notice how the legs are bent through contact and the follow-through and how the shoulders continue to open up.

6

The follow-through is on a horizontal plane and the racquet points approx-imately toward the right wall on the finish. Make sure your body stays low.

KEY ELEMENTS OF THE SWING

Think "Shoulder Action"

Just as you can salvage your forehand with a proper wrist snap, you can generate real power on the backhand with a smooth, solid rotation by your hitting shoulder (plus a little help from your hips).

I recently worked with a woman in San Diego who didn't have any real power—or confidence—in her backhand until I started telling her, "Hit it with your *shoulder*—not your racquet. The racquet's a necessary evil; it has to be there. But you actually want to hit the ball by having your shoulder come through solidly as the racquet just trails along at the end." When I hit the ball to her, I made sure she had her racquet pulled back for a full swing, and then I'd say, "Shoulder!" And she would just concentrate on turning her shoulders into the shot. If she went after the ball too early, I'd say, "Wait on the ball and shoulder it." Pretty soon the ball was just popping off her racquet. She wasn't bending her legs—that was our next goal—and yet she was generating good velocity just with the uncoiling of her upper body and a little rotation of her hips.

Physiologically, in fact, the backhand is actually an easier motion than the forehand because the body opens up naturally as you uncoil your hitting shoulder; there's nothing to impede your swing as you drive into the ball and then follow through.

"Get Ready Early–Then Wait "

When you set up for your shot, tell yourself to "take the racquet back quickly—and then wait." This will help you avoid a short, punching stroke in two ways:

1. By having your racquet up in its cocked position—instead of pulled in against your chest—you can bring your hitting shoulder down through the ball with authority.

2. By getting ready early and then waiting on the ball—much like a baseball hitter—you maximize the coordination and power in your shoulder swing.

Many people have a tendency to jump at the ball, instead of letting it come to them. They're unsure of their swing and they feel uncomfortable about letting the ball get too close; they're afraid they aren't going to be able to get their racquet around in time. They also have such a fear that the ball is going to bounce twice in front of them, or is going to get by them into the corners, that they just reach out and punch at the ball.

1

In waiting for a backhand, start with your racquet carried around knee-high, with the wrist fairly relaxed. Then as you move toward the ball, bring your racquet up around waist or shoulder level. This helps ensure a quick, flowing motion as you pull the racquet back up into its cocked position.

Getting Good Direction

Your eventual goal on the backhand is to be able to bang that ball into the front left corner so that it either goes for a kill or a down-the-wall passing shot. This ability will force your opponent to respect your left-wall play, and you thus keep him more centrally located so he can't overplay your shots.

Therefore, learn to step at a 45° angle into the left wall and funnel your stroke toward the front corner. But swing freely. Don't try to "aim" the ball or guide it there with a forced stroke.

Getting Low

You can develop a good backhand stroke without much bending of your legs—providing you compensate properly. You must master a good shoulder rotation (since you're losing power by failing to utilize your lower body in the swing), and you need to make the right adjustments to get your racquet down to the level of the ball. This means bending over at the waist and dipping down with your hitting shoulder. The more you can bend your knees comfortably, the less you will have to make these adjustments, and thus the fewer errors you should make in driving the ball low into the front wall.

The Hitting Arm

As you develop a swing with good shoulder action, your hitting arm will find a comfortable path to take—far enough away from your body to allow your hitting shoulder to come through unrestricted, yet not so far away that you acquire a tennis stroke. For a checkpoint, your elbow should be about six to ten inches from your body at impact.

The Wrist

There are two ways to cock the wrist when you have your racquet in a set position. But then the action of the wrist is pretty much standarized. Either way you start out, the wrist will remain cocked until it snaps forcibly through that 12-to-18-inch range before impact. But as soon as it completes its snap, then hold it and keep it fixed—if you let it roll over or just flick at the ball, then your shots will spray in every direction.

1

There are two ways to cock your wrist in the set position. The conventional method (1) has your wrist cocked up, in direct line with the forearm. This requires less movement by the wrist as you start your swing, and it leads to better consistency by the average player. Some players, however, like to curl the wrist back (2). This allows for a longer wrist extension and more of a whipping action, and thus can generate a little more velocity on the ball. But it requires *expert* timing.

2

THE BACKHAND WRIST SNAP

The wrist is fully cocked.   The wrist starts to extend before contact.

The wrist is snapping more, and the racquet is coming through on a horizontal plane.

At contact, the wrist finishes its snapping motion.

At the beginning of the follow-through, the wrist is held firm and the racquet is still horizontal.

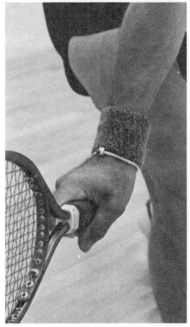

Notice the continuous firm hold of the wrist. This firm wrist position after contact will give maximum direction to your shot.

Notice the *improper* rolling of the wrist after contact. Rolling over the ball like this will tend to send your shots into the floor.

The Non-Hitting Arm

A lot of tennis converts like to place their left hand on the throat of their racquet as they draw it back, but this can be destructive in learning a proper racquetball backhand. It prevents you from bringing the racquet back far enough and quick enough so that you can take a full swing at the ball, and it leads instead to a short, punching stroke.

Another question is what to do with the non-hitting arm. By practicing and experimenting, you'll find the position that's comfortable and efficient for you. I used to play with my left arm held tightly against my body (against my thigh or in next to my side), but now I'm learning to hold it out away because I think the added clearance gives me a quicker swing with more potential power. The key thing is that your left arm should benefit your balance and help you swing with a fluid motion. You don't want it positioned so that it takes away from the full extension of that swing.

The Follow-Through

After contacting the ball, and with the wrist held firm, you want to pull through with your hitting shoulder so that the racquet travels on as horizontal a plane as possible. This will enable you to have greater consistency in keeping the ball low on the front wall. If your shots keep hitting too high on the front wall, then either your follow-through is carrying up too high or your racquet face is beveled (tilted) up at impact, instead of being straight up and down.

THE OPEN-STANCE SWING 1

Due to the speed of the shot, you have a shortened backswing and very little rotation of the shoulders. Your feet are wide apart so you have a powerful base of support.

2

The knees are slightly bent and the racquet is coming through on a horizontal plane. There's no time for the hitter to step into the ball, so he must hit from a stationary position.

3

Contact is made off the front foot, the wrist has snapped, and the body has remained low.

4

The body continues to stay low, the wrist is held firm, and the follow-through is shortened.

COMMON BACKHAND ERRORS

Placing your left hand on the racquet handle will prevent your racquet from being pulled back to its proper set position, and it will inhibit you from having a fluid swing. Notice the lack of shoulder rotation by the hitter.

This is a similar problem, with the racquet not pulled back properly. Insufficient knee bend and excessive bending at the waist will also place the hitter in trouble.

3

The knees are not bent and the racquet is too low in its set position. This resembles a two-handed tennis backhand, which is not what you want.

4

A basically good swing is ruined by having the racquet face tilted upward at impact. The ball can go only in one direction—high up on the front wall.

PRACTICING THE BACKHAND

Use the same drills described in the forehand (page 70). If you're unable to hit a backhand up to the front wall that returns to your backhand side, then start your drills by lobbing a forehand so that you can simply turn around and hit a backhand.

As you're gaining confidence in this stroke, just practice hitting it up and down the left wall, about 3 feet high or lower. You'll have trouble keeping the ball off the left wall and out of center court, but remember: the people you are playing at your ability level are also having a tough time with this shot. So you want to learn to direct the ball into their weakness as much as you can.

Once you acquire a dependable stroke, you can start rallying with yourself completely on the left side of the court, and eventually you can practice cutting the ball off near the front court. But this will take a good, firm stroke that sends the ball into the front wall with accuracy and velocity.

This sequence shows that common backhand ailment—the punch stroke. In the first photo, the hitting arm is held too far away from the body. Then, at contact, the racquet is still too far away from the body, thus placing all of the strain of the swing on the hitting arm. The follow-through is equally wasted as far as generating any power. The entire swing lacks wrist snap and good shoulder power.

1

2

3

BACKHAND FUNDAMENTALS

1. Have your racquet set quickly, and pulled back.

2. Have your wrist in a cocked position to help ensure an explosive wrist snap.

3. Your legs should be comfortably bent to help generate a more total body swing.

4. Have your left arm positioned so you have clearance to swing freely.

5. Let the ball come to you so you can take a full shoulder swing.

6. Rotate your shoulders toward the back wall.

7. Uncoil your hitting shoulder and your hips into the ball so that your racquet can move freely through impact. There should be a natural opening-up of the body.

8. Don't be tentative; get the racquet back as you set up, and then bring that hitting shoulder down through the ball with force.

9. Strong shoulders will help, but flexibility is just as important to enable your upper body to rotate easily.

10. Let your body do its work before your racquet contacts the ball.

11. Snap the wrist forcibly through contact, but don't let it roll over; let the hitting shoulder pull the racquet through.

12. Follow through at about waist level.

13. Poking the ball will result in a weak, incomplete follow-through.

14. Try to funnel your strokes down into the left front corner. But first strive for velocity. You want to at least put pressure on your opponent to make the next play when you miss your target. A short, punching stroke will give him too many setups.

CHAPTER 6

GOOD RACQUETBALL SHOTS

This chapter will detail the shots you need in order to play a good all-around game of racquetball. Each shot has the potential to help you gain and maintain center-court positioning, or to keep your opponent guessing at your intentions. But each shot also has inherent flaws, and only through experience will you learn which ones you should rely on under pressure.

THE KILL SHOT

Once a rally is under way, you want to go for the kill attempt whenever you have an offensive opportunity. Among the different-angled shots that can result in an outright winner are:

1. The "roll-out" — a ball that actually rolls along the floor after it hits the front wall.

2. Any ball hit straight into the front wall that takes two quick bounces before your opponent can reach it.

3. A pinch shot that hits low and tight into the front corner.

4. A cross-court shot that bounces twice before it reaches your opponent (known as a cross-court kill).

5. A shot that angles off the front wall and nicks the side wall, but which is hit so low that it is irretrievable on two bounces.

6. An overhead that hits directly into the front corner on a perfect angle.

Your decision to go for a kill shot will be influenced by where your opponent is located on the court, his or her retrieving ability, the height at which the ball is coming to you, your readiness to play the ball offensively, your own ability level, and common tactical sense. For example, when your opponent is obviously out of position, why risk a 6-inch-high kill attempt that can easily ''skip'' into the floor when a 24-inch passing shot can be just as effective in ending the rally?

In general, these are good kill-shot situations:

● When you have time to set up for the shot and you are within your reasonable scoring range.

● When you are in center court and you know your opponent is behind you.

● When your opponent hits a ceiling ball that comes in short.

● When the ball rebounds off the back wall into your scoring range.

The reason kill attempts are so important is that they often put your opponent in trouble even when they fail. For instance, a straight-in kill attempt along one of the side walls may hit higher than you intended on the front wall, but it may result in a successful down-the-wall pass. Even if it goes to your opponent in center court directly off the front wall, the velocity of the ball will demand a good ''reflex'' stroke.

This is why I like beginners to take the offensive whenever possible. Their kill attempts may keep funneling into the middle of the court, but their opponents are going to lack the ability to capitalize on these scoring opportunities, and they may very often return the ball for a setup.

One warning, however, about a *missed pinch shot:* if the ball strikes higher than about 2 feet in the front corner, or on too wide an angle off the side wall, then it angles directly into the middle of the court as a ''plum'' shot. But as you play better racquetball, you can't back off from the pinch. This is such an effective shot from center court that it has to be taken, despite the risk involved.

PASSING SHOTS

Good passing shots, whether hit by design or as the result of a missed kill attempt, are crucial to successful center-court play. You want to go for the kill shot whenever a scoring situation arises, but passing shots are needed to keep your attack diversified and your opponent off balance. The more you can drive the ball up and down a side wall, or cross-

The cross-court pass can either: (a) hit the floor and then go straight into the back corner or glance off the side wall (photo 1) or (b) hit the side wall in the air after hitting the front wall (photo 2). You must keep both of these shots from rebounding off the *back* wall.

court—*and keep it from rebounding off the back wall*—the less your opponent can relax and overplay the middle of the court. You want to force him to stretch out to the perimeters of his comfortable hitting zone—and beyond—while you gain center-court control.

When you are aiming specifically for a down-the-wall pass, the two crucial factors are: (1) hit the ball low enough to keep it from rebounding off the back wall and (2) don't let it rebound off the side wall, unless it hits a side wall *behind* your opponent. This shot will kick into the deep middle of the court and die before it hits the back wall.

In going cross-court, again keep the ball low into the front wall, and remember your geometry. To drive a ball from anywhere on the court so that it travels diagonally into a back corner, your target is virtually the *center of the front wall,* or slightly to either side. The closer you hit toward a side wall, the more your shot is going to angle into that side wall and kick back into center court.

It's easy to be fooled by the angles involved in hitting passing shots, or not to realize what is actually happening as you play. Therefore, try to get on an empty court and test the angles for yourself. Stand in different parts of the court, bounce the ball, and then see where you actually must strike the front wall—and at what height—to produce successful passing shots.

VOLLEYING

If you're determined to maintain good center-court positioning, you must learn to volley the ball as it comes to you in the air, at *about waist level or below*. You may be tempted to let these balls travel into the back wall for a rebound shot, but in doing so you give up control of center court, and you hit from a deeper position. By holding your ground and going for the volley, you keep the pressure on your opponent, and you can save four or five steps, thus conserving energy while playing better racquetball.

However, in your eagerness to play the game offensively, don't try to volley a ball that is coming off the front wall at about *chest level or above*. This is a difficult shot to return low into the front wall, so let it go by. It will hit the back wall on one hard bounce or in the air and rebound into center court for a "plum." When your opponent's shot arrives in that gray area between waist and chest level, go for the volley only if you're efficient with this shot and you have a capable swing. Otherwise, it doesn't pay to take chances until you improve your stroke.

1

TYPICAL VOLLEY SITUATIONS

The player on the right has hit a shot that angles into her opponent's fore-hand. His two options with a volley are: (1) pinch the ball into the right corner; (2) cross-court the ball down the left wall.

2

3

The player on the right has hit a low-drive shot to her opponent's backhand. His options on the volley are: (1) pinch the ball into the left corner; (2) drive the ball up and down the left wall, away from his opponent.

4

The Stroke

You may at first be intimidated by the volley. The ball's coming pretty fast off the front wall and you think the stroke is going to be too difficult to master. Yet once you acquire the basics, the ball's velocity will work in your behalf.

First, *be ready to volley* so you can set up quickly with good balance. Make that mental transition to where you anticipate every volley opportunity, instead of being caught by surprise.

Second, have a short, compact, relatively open-stanced swing. You want to sacrifice power in favor of accuracy this close to the front wall (21 to 28 feet away).

Third, *tighten your grip at impact* so that you make solid contact. If your racquet is held weakly, the speed of the ball will twist the racquet in your hand.

Fourth, keep your eyes on the ball and stay down through the shot.

Shot Strategy

Approach the volley with enthusiasm, because it offers you an excellent chance to win the point outright or to force your opponent into a weak return.

Your initial goal is to direct your volley into the nearest front corner, about 0 to 10 inches high, so that one of several shots can result: the straight-in kill, a tight pinch, or a down-the-wall pass. Try to score; don't play defensively by simply driving the ball 3 feet high. *You're volleying to maintain dominance, and to hopefully win the point—not just to keep the ball in play.*

By forcing your opponent to cover more kill attempts and passing shots, you reduce his effectiveness in two important ways. First, he doesn't get as many opportunities, or as much time, to set up properly for his next shot. Second, when you are a constant threat to either pinch the ball for a kill or go down-the-wall for a pass, your opponent is always in limbo, never knowing if he's going to have to thrust forward or move quickly to one side. He has barely completed his follow-through and now he must commit himself before he really might want to move. That's a tough way to play.

Practicing the Volley

It's hard to practice the volley as an isolated stroke, since most players lack the accuracy to drive the ball into the front wall so that it comes back to them in the air, between the knees and the waist. Instead, what you must do is practice about three different shots at once from a position near the front of center court.

(1) If the ball comes to you for a volley, work on getting down so that you drive the ball as low and on as straight a line as possible into the front wall. (2) When the ball bounces to you off the front wall, don't let it go by; cut it off and hit the same scoring shots you took on the volley. And (3), when the ball arrives around chest level or above, just let it go by and get ready to practice your shot off the back wall.

THE CEILING SHOT

Your defensive approach to racquetball should be as offensive as possible. In other words, when your opponent controls center court and forces you to hit from the perimeter, don't automatically take the defensive; try to hit aggressive shots that can shift the pressure onto your opponent and enable you to regain a share of center court.

However, when you are in such a precarious position that you feel you can't hit an offensive shot without giving your opponent a "plum" in the middle, then *go to the ceiling*. This is your best-percentage defensive shot, and it can even be a smart offensive play against certain players.

You'll normally hit this shot from deep back court, aiming for a ceiling

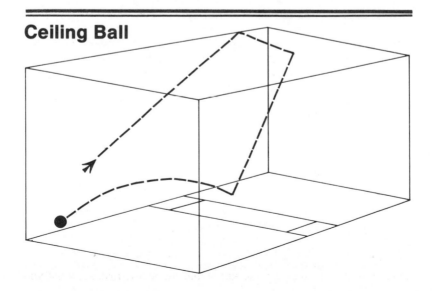

Ceiling Ball

target about 3 feet from the front wall. The ball will then carom into the front wall and take its first bounce around the service zone area and finally locate very near the back wall. This forces your opponent out of center court, and it presents him with a high-bouncing ball about head-high that is difficult to return offensively.

Try to direct your ceiling shots into your opponent's backhand corner, since this is usually his weakest area. In average play, if you can then hit the ball so that it hugs the side wall coming down, this can force your opponent into an error as he tries to scrape the ball off the wall. But if you consistently hit into the wall on too much of an angle and the ball pops out for a "plum," then simply aim safely for the middle of the court.

If you're going to error on this shot, make sure you at least hit the ceiling. When you hit too far back on the ceiling, the ball doesn't carry as deep, but it still forces your opponent to hit from 30 to 35 feet. Whereas if you miss the ceiling completely and hit the front wall 15 to 18 feet high, that ball's probably going to rebound off the back wall in the air and travel into the front-court area, where your opponent will be waiting to end the rally.

The Ceiling-Ball Rally

When you hit a successful ceiling ball, there's very little your opponent can do with the shot except to go back to the ceiling. If he, too, brings the ball back deep, then you should try to prolong what is known as a ceiling rally. Both of you will remain near the back wall and exchange ceiling balls until one of you errors by hitting the ball weakly, or long off the back wall. This person will then move into a center-court position and try to cover his opponent's scoring opportunity.

After hitting a good ceiling ball, always stay back with your opponent. There's no reason for you to hustle into center court to cover his possible offensive shots, since your shot should force him to go back to the ceiling. If you get into a ceiling-ball rally, it's better to avoid many kill attempts, "Z" balls, around-the-wall balls, or overhead kills (which will be explained in the following pages). They're very difficult to execute from this deep on the court, and they usually lead to more points for your opponent rather than benefit you.

THE FOREHAND CEILING SHOT

When the ball is bouncing high, up around your head, visualize a motion in which you are throwing your racquet over a neighbor's fence. In the first picture, notice how the racquet is cocked up behind the head and that the knees are slightly bent for balance. Then study the sequence to see how easily you want to swing at the ball. The ceiling shot is basically a direction shot hit with moderate force. (If the ball bounces to you around waist to chest level so quickly that you can't hit an effective kill or pass, use a sidearm type of swing to jam the ball up to the ceiling.)

THE BACKHAND CEILING SHOT

You actually want to use your fundamental backhand stroke, except that you swing up at the ball on a slight angle. In the first photo, the racquet is held up behind the head and the hitting shoulder is slightly rotated. In the second and third photos, notice the step toward the side wall on about a 45-degree angle and the hitting motion of the shoulder. Ball contact is made with the racquet directing the ball to the ceiling, and the follow-through is a natural motion of the hitting shoulder.

THE OVERHEAD

This shot is too risky and too difficult to master for it to ever become a consistent offensive weapon. But good players use it as a change-of-pace alternative to the ceiling shot.

There are two types of overheads — the drive and the kill — and both are hit with basically the same motion as the ceiling ball, except that the face of the racquet is tilted at different angles into the front wall at impact instead of up into the ceiling. Visualize a ball-throwing motion, or the overhead stroke in tennis in which you take the racquet back at about eye level and then hit through the ball. (The overhead may become a better percentage shot in the future as players grow more familiar with the hitting motion, but today it seems a natural stroke only to those with a tennis or badminton background.)

The Overhead Drive

You really only want to use this stroke when you've been driven into the deep back court by a ceiling shot or any high-bouncing ball. Instead of going to the ceiling (and either initiating or prolonging a ceiling rally), you may want to try an overhead straight into the front wall, about 3 or 4 feet high, so that the ball does one of two things:

(1) It goes down the side wall and forces your opponent out of center court and into the back corner.

(2) It takes its first bounce around the service zone area and comes up into your opponent's body, forcing a tough return.

On both shots you want to take off enough velocity so the ball won't come off the back wall and allow your opponent to set up for a kill attempt. You also take these shots with the realization that your odds are better with the ceiling ball, and that it doesn't pay to take this gamble unless you have a good strategic reason, *i.e.,* you want to force your opponent out of a ceiling-ball rally and get him to play a faster-paced game.

The Overhead Kill

This is an even more difficult shot than the overhead drive, because you're shooting from around head level and trying to angle the ball down into a front corner as low as possible so that the ball takes two quick bounces for a kill. It's great when you have the timing and the touch, but when your accuracy is just slightly off, you hit losers.

The time to use this shot is during a ceiling rally, when your opponent is positioned alongside you in front of the back wall. Since you use the same hitting motion on the overhead as you do for the ceiling, you can camouflage your intentions until the ball actually leaves your racquet. Then if your opponent gets careless and is automatically expecting the ceiling ball—or if he tends to be a bit lazy—your overhead can force him to thrust forward toward the front court, and very often he won't reach the ball in time.

THE "Z" BALL

You can use this frenzied-looking shot to surprise your opponent or to "buy time" while you scramble back into play. But it must be hit sparingly to be effective.

The "Z" gets its name because of the pattern it traces off the walls. It strikes the front wall about 15 or 16 feet high in the corner and quickly caroms off the side wall with enough force to carry diagonally cross-court. Then it rebounds off that side wall—about 2 or 3 feet from the back wall—and travels virtually parallel to the back wall, thus presenting a potentially difficult shot to return.

The "Z" confuses inexperienced players because they're not accustomed to playing a ball that is angling sideways. The proximity of the back wall also tends to inhibit their swing. But once they see a few "Z's" and figure out the ball's pattern, they feel a lot more comfortable. Instead of wondering where the ball is going to end up, they know they can move into position in the back part of the court and wait for the ball to come to them off the side wall. Still, a good stroke is required to hit the ball offensively to the front wall.

When shooting the "Z," don't let all the different angles worry you. If you can hit the correct front-wall target area—with pretty good force—then geometry will take over and carry the ball back deep so that it slides along the back wall. The "Z" is also useful for breaking up a specific pattern of play, and for when you have to stretch or dive for the ball and you know you're going to need time to scramble back into center court. You can regain the middle while your opponent waits for the ball to ricochet about the walls.

"Z" Ball

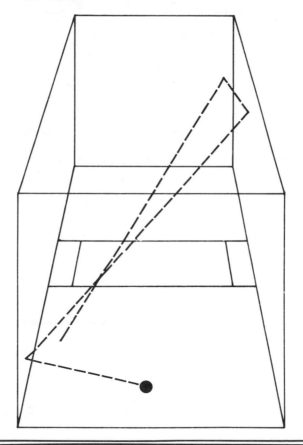

"AROUND-THE-WALL BALL"

This is a cousin of the "Z" ball, and it's pretty easy to execute, but it doesn't have much value beyond generating a different type of rally and being employed as a change of pace. It's the type of shot you want your opponent to try, because the ball always travels across center court, even when perfectly hit.

Unlike the "Z," you want the "ATWB" to contact a side wall first (about 12 to 15 feet high, relative to where you are hitting), at about 3 feet from the front wall. The ball will then rebound off the front wall and travel cross-court to the opposite side wall, where it rebounds sharply and heads on a diagonal toward the back corner, taking its first bounce about two-thirds of the way across the court.

The best way to defend against the "ATWB" is to learn to cut the ball off *in the air* as it angles across center court. If you let it bounce, it angles into deep court and you'll end up returning the ball from 38 feet.

"SOFT" SHOTS

When you hustle into the front court for a missed shot by your opponent, and you're tempted to hit a little "soft" shot to end the rally, be aware that this requires the kind of touch most pros wish they had. You have to suddenly ease off to hit the ball while you're still on the move, and the tendency is to either guide the ball into the floor for a "skip," or to leave it too high on the front wall.

Another problem with this shot is that there's virtually no middle ground. If you fail to hit an outright winner—by hitting the ball low enough into your opponent's front corner so that he or she can't retrieve it—then look out: you may not get another shot. A competent opponent will simply rush in and make the play. In my opinion, that's too great a penalty to pay for such a slight error in accuracy against the front wall. You're much smarter to hit a kill attempt or a low drive, which, if hit too high, will at least come back to your opponent with good velocity.

Nevertheless, there are times when you can use the "soft" shot to good advantage, but only at the right moment and against the right opponent. If your match is being played at such a hard, fast pace that you sense your opponent is back on his heels, anticipating another ball pounding off that front wall, then a well-executed "soft" shot may catch him off guard. Similarly, a player whose concentration is suspect, who has slow reactions, or who lacks the ability to thrust forward quickly is fair game. Just keep in mind that your success with this shot will increase proportionally the closer you get to the front wall and the farther back your opponent is positioned.

Around-the-Wall-Ball

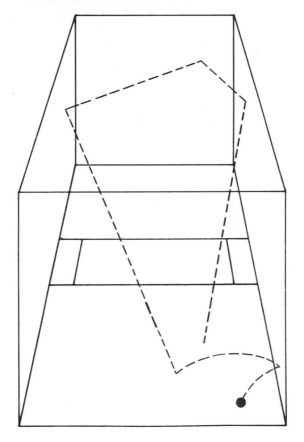

1

THE "SOFT" SHOT

The hitter tries to "dump" the ball into a front corner, hitting with a guiding motion and a flat follow-through. Notice how the knees are bent, thus allowing the hitter to push through the ball with a straight racquet. As easy as this stroke might appear to be, it requires perfect touch to produce a winning shot.

2

CHAPTER 7

PLAYING THE SIDE WALLS AND THE BACK WALL

Newcomers to racquetball who have a little athletic ability and a grasp of center-court strategy may feel pretty confident when they go out to play their first match. But as soon as the ball starts caroming off side walls and taking fiendish bounces in the back corners, they realize the game is not quite as easy as they envisioned. In fact, it can take five or six matches to learn how to be comfortable with that ricocheting ball and how to "play" it properly as it reacts off the side walls and the back wall. This chapter will give you the important fundamentals that should speed your familiarity—and your progress.

The Side Walls

When you see the ball heading for a side wall, try to keep two related thoughts in mind: (1) remember your geometry and the angles the ball can take; (2) let the ball rebound off the wall to you.

Most beginners forget how lively the ball is, and that even the slightest glancing blow off the side wall will send it back near the middle of the court. Thus, they often charge over so close to the wall that the ball jams against their body and forces them to take a weak, punching stroke. Sometimes they get so overeager that they swing and miss, fooled by how the ball angles off.

To avoid these common problems, try to move quickly into position on the perimeter of the center-court area—safely away from the wall—so that you can swing comfortably wherever the ball rebounds. Pull your racquet up in a cocked, ready position, and then let the ball react off the wall before you commit yourself.

Your body should be facing the side wall at about a 45-degree angle to allow you a good look at the ball as it comes toward you. Then you can rotate your shoulders slightly, and use your strong, quick stroke. Have your legs comfortably bent so that you are ready for any situation that might arise. If you've misjudged the ball, you can adjust and move quickly. If you've judged it right, then the bent legs will make for a better swing. But when you're in a high, stiff-legged position, you'll find it difficult to thrust out wide or low for the ball without losing your balance.

This solid ready position will also enable you to react confidently— rather than with panic—when a hard-hit ball is "hugging" the side wall on a passing shot, or you sense that it is barely going to skim off the wall. There's no time to worry whether the ball is going to hit the racquet a split-second before it contacts the wall, or a split-second after. All you can do is try to scrape the ball off the wall the best you can.

PLAYING THE SIDE WALL

Notice how the hitter sets up for a ball that is sliding along the right wall. He takes a normal forehand swing and the racquet virtually scrapes the ball off the wall. Players have to overcome the psychological barrier of not taking a full swing because of the proximity of the wall.

1   **2**

3

4

The Back Wall

Although the back wall can pose problems at first, you'll find that it's the easiest wall to play once you learn to judge how far the ball is going to rebound, and how to get into the right stroking position. Then it's a matter of simply hitting a ball that's already on its way to the front wall, instead of having to reverse the ball's direction.

The first crucial step in learning to play the back wall is to develop a sense of how far your opponent's shot is going to travel after it rebounds off the front wall. Will the ball carry into the back wall on one bounce? Or in the air? (Experience will fill more gaps in your mind that anything else, but you should also review the rules of thumb described in the section on the volley, page 107.)

When you're positioned in center court and you know your opponent's shot has enough velocity and height to carry into the back wall *in the air,* then stay where you are and wait for the ball to come back into your area. For example, if you're 22 feet from the front wall, there's no need to retreat, since the ball is going to rebound near to where you are standing, and oftentimes even forward of that. With experience, you'll learn to move into the specific area where you expect the ball to bounce, and to position yourself so that as the ball goes past your body and drops low, you can contact it from behind and slam it straight into the front wall for a kill attempt.

If the ball rebounds into the back wall *on one bounce,* it can carry 3 to 20 feet toward the front court, depending upon velocity. But in any case, you want to move back with the ball as it heads for the back wall so that when it rebounds out, you're *behind* the ball, ready to take a short but forceful stroke. Remember, you have to contact this shot before it hits the floor again. Try to get a rhythm going where you tell yourself, "Go back with the ball, and come out with the ball." You get more power and accuracy with this type of approach to your stroke.

In playing the ball as it rebounds off the floor into the back wall, incorporate these other tips:

● Hustle back with long, shuffle-type steps so you're ready to set up quickly.

● Make sure you retreat far enough to come back out with the ball. If it rebounds farther than you anticipated, it's much easier—and certainly more offensive—to move quickly forward than it is to reach back toward the back wall to take a weak, flicking type of stroke.

● Let the ball drop to between knee and ankle height so that you can drive it low and straight into the front wall, on the side from which you are hitting. Avoid pinch shots, since your opponent should be waiting in center court for any error you make in hitting the side wall.

In practicing your back-wall shots in general, there are two stages.

First, you want to get accustomed to the stroking pattern and the timing involved. The easiest method is to stand about 4 or 5 feet from the back wall and then just lob the ball into the wall with your left hand. Let the ball go past you toward the front wall, and then move up and blast it with a flat, hard swing. Work on that rhythm of moving out with the ball as it comes off the wall and then making contact as it drops low.

Second, once you're comfortable with the stroke, stand in center court and drive the ball into the front wall so that you can work on the total sequence: judging how far the ball is going to carry into the back wall, positioning yourself on the court in relationship with the ball, and then taking your stroke.

Beginners and intermediates should work particularly hard on back-wall shots because they will occur repeatedly during their matches. Opponents at their level of ability will simply hit the ball too high into the front wall, too often.

PLAYING OFF THE BACK WALL

1   2

3

4

When the ball is bouncing into the back wall, you want to retreat quickly so that you can come out with the ball as it rebounds forward. Notice in this sequence how the hitter has his racquet pulled back as the ball comes off the back wall, and then he takes two quick shuffle steps to build up momentum before hitting the ball. He uses a regular forehand stroke and has a natural follow-through.

5

THE BACK CORNERS

It can take a long time to acquire the skill—and the confidence—to retrieve shots that travel into the deep back corners, and to then return the ball to the front wall with more than a hope and a prayer. But this is an ability you need to have to consistently beat other players. They will try to make the ball die in the back corners with cross-court and down-the-wall passes (and, as we shall see, with virtually every serve). Fortunately, it's difficult to make the ball locate in these corners for an outright winner. Unfortunately, near-misses are virtually as effective. The ball can easily "freak," or rebound, or bounce in odd directions when it gets into where the two walls meet. Plus, you don't have long to react, since the ball must be contacted before it hits the floor. It's also easy to be inhibited and actually cramped as you try to dig the ball out with the best stroke you can muster, a foot or two away from the walls.

To improve your chances when you go into the back corners, start by carrying your racquet up around chest level so that you can quickly bring it up into a ready position. Second, bend your legs and stay low so you have a better chance of reacting to the weird rebounds or bounces the ball might take out of the corner. Even the pros are jammed or fooled by a ball that "freaks" in a different direction than they anticipated, or jumps right into them. Third, when you manage to get your racquet on the ball, your best shot will be to go to the ceiling. If this isn't possible, then hit whatever shot will get the ball back to the front wall and keep the rally alive. Here's where that quick snap of the wrist on the forehand, and a quick forceful shoulder swing on the backhand, may save you.

CHAPTER 8

THE SERVE

The serve is your most important weapon, and the one over which you have the most control. Starting from scratch, you can learn to serve effectively—in a relatively short period of time—by hitting the basic front-wall target areas shown in this chapter. And if you can then relocate properly just behind the service zone, you will automatically control center court.

Some of you may be thinking: "I've only played twice. How can I learn a good serve when I don't even have good strokes yet?" Don't let your mind inhibit you. You're forgetting the built-in advantages the server has: (1) you control the ball you're hitting—by bouncing the ball in front of you, at the height you want—while your opponent must react to a ball that is either moving low and hard, bouncing high, or glancing quickly off side walls; (2) you're contacting the ball only 16 to 17 feet from the front wall, but your opponent must move and then hit from 36 to 38 feet away, if you serve properly; (3) when you relocate correctly, the pressure is on your opponent to kill the return or hit the shot that drives you out of center court.

So if you're just starting out in this game, or you're an intermediate who has never really known *where* to aim your serves, try to memorize this chapter—and practice—until you can visualize your front-wall targets in your sleep. Right away you're going to force your opponents to play good racquetball if they hope to regain the serve.

These are the front-wall targets you want to strive to hit from near the middle of the service zone. This photograph puts the ceiling, the floor, and the targets in proportion so you can see how high the target boxes actually are.

THE BASIC SERVES

There are four basic serves—the low-drive, the "Z," the half-lob and the high-lob. Your goal on all of them is to direct the ball into one of the back corners so that it takes its second bounce into an imaginary box that extends about 3 feet in from the side wall and 5 feet forward of the back wall. This gives your opponent a difficult shot to return offensively and enables you to reposition in center court.

The Low-Drive Serve

This is your power serve, and it is probably the most common of all the serves. Contact the ball with a regular wrist-snapping forehand stroke and try to drive it just past the short line so that it skips as low as possible into the back corner. Your opponent must then move quickly, set up instantly, and execute properly to keep from hitting a "plum" to you in center court.

The server should contact the ball near the middle of the service zone. The returnee normally stands in the middle of the court, about two strides away from the back wall.

A crucial point here, and on all the serves you hit: *keep the ball from bouncing off the back wall,* since this will give your opponent a much easier return. This means your low-drive serve must hit the front wall about 3 feet or lower, assuming reasonable velocity.

The angle at which you hit the front wall will sometimes result in your serve striking the floor and then nicking the side wall on its way to the back corner. Hit low and hard, this serve will give your opponent trouble by caroming quickly off the wall, providing it stays close to the wall. However, an important warning: don't let this serve glance off the side wall in the air *before* hitting the floor, because it will simply angle directly into the deep middle of the court and give your opponent an offensive opportunity. (One exception to the rule: if you can hit the "crack" where the side wall meets the floor, the ball will "roll out" for an ace.)

The "Z" Serve

This is an important serve which, when properly executed, can cause your opponent considerable grief in the back corners of the court. The stroking pattern is generally the same as on the low-drive serve, except that you're angling the ball into the front corner. The ball strikes the front wall about 5 to 6 feet off the floor, and about 9 to 12 inches from the side wall. It then caroms quickly off that wall, cuts diagonally across the court, strikes the floor, and then ricochets off the wall—thus tracing a "Z" pattern. This forces your opponent to set up quickly and hit the ball before it returns to the floor for its second bounce.

Some players use the "Z" as an ace attempt on the first serve by having it get deep in the back corner or having it "freak" along the side and back walls. But more often it is employed as an effective second serve, when you want control and accuracy rather than outright velocity. The "Z" may *appear* too dangerous and complicated to rely on under pressure—having to hit all those walls and the floor in the right sequence—but remember: once you strike your front-wall target correctly, geometry takes over and the ball will always locate properly in that back-corner "box" (which on the "Z" is 3 or 4 feet wider, with the same depth). In fact, with a little practice and experience, you'll find that the "Z" is as easy to hit accurately as the low-drive.

Of course, there are dangers. If you hit the front wall on too wide an angle (too far from the side wall), then the ball will rebound into the back wall and come out as an easy setup. Or if you hit too tight a pinch into the front corner, the ball will rebound off the opposite side wall short of the back wall for a scoring opportunity.

Low-Drive Serve

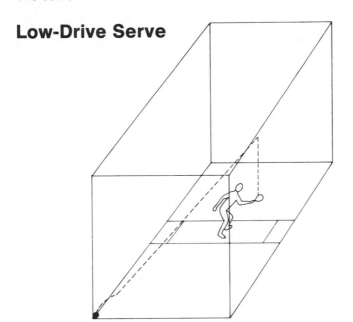

"Z" Serve

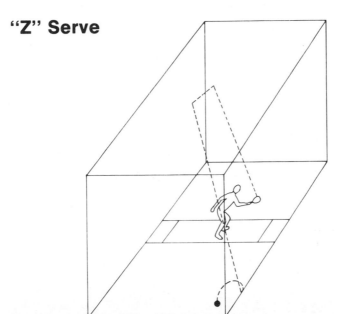

Half-Lob Serve

When you want to generate a slower-paced game, or you sense that your opponent is getting used to your hard-velocity serves, then try an off-speed serve like the half-lob. Properly hit (with much less force than the low-drive or "Z"), the half-lob will strike the front wall, rebound two or three feet beyond the back service line, and then carry deep toward the back corner. This forces your opponent to contact the ball at around shoulder height, before he's constricted by the back wall. Since it's difficult to kill a 4- or 5-foot-high ball from that distance, the only reasonable return is a ceiling shot. But if your opponent has been seeing nothing but hard serves, a sudden half-lob might look so inviting that he goes for an offensive return. And in his eagerness to flatten the ball, he often ends up over-swinging or swinging too early—to your benefit.

When you stroke the half-lob, forget all about a wrist snap, since direction is what you want, not velocity. Keep your hitting arm bent, but tighten up your wrist, as you might in tennis, and concentrate on a compact hitting motion. *But don't give yourself away.* If you fail to camouflage your intention, an alert opponent will rush up and cut the ball off in the air, and he'll either hit a kill attempt or a passing shot. Also remember to keep the ball from hitting a side wall on its way to the back corner. The ball is already traveling so slowly that your opponent would be able to really tee-off.

This is a good second serve, since it's pretty easy to hit with good accuracy—providing you get out and practice.

The High-Lob Serve

Like the half-lob, this is a carefully directed serve that requires an accurate touch. But it is used commonly in club and tournament play to start a slower-paced rally, since it gives one's opponent a difficult shot to hit solidly to the front wall.

Utilize the same bent-armed swing as on the half-lob, but angle the ball off the front wall so that it *hits the side wall on the descent* into the back court. (When you practice this shot without an opponent on the court, try to have the ball "die" in the back corner before it comes off the back wall.) The danger in this serve is that if the ball comes up short, or fails to hit the side wall, your opponent will be able to cut it off and hit an offensive return, forcing you to react and move quickly in the direction of the shot.

Half-Lob Serve

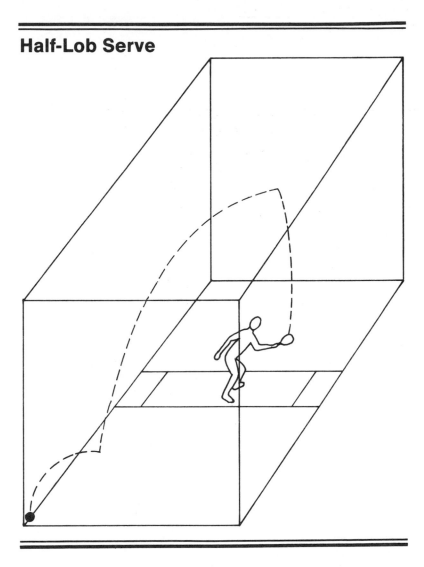

High-Lob Serve

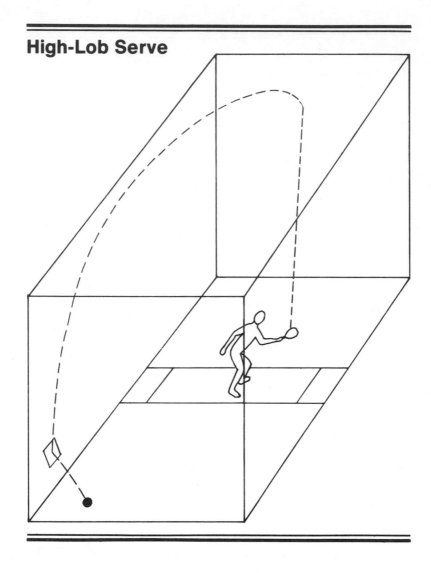

POSITIONING IN THE SERVICE ZONE

Regardless of where your opponent is waiting to return the serve, *standardize your serving position in the middle of the service zone,* or just slightly to one side, so that you contact the ball midway between the two side walls. This (1) maximizes the number of effective serves you can hit; (2) camouflages the direction of your intended serve much more effectively; (3) helps groove your memory of those front-court targets. Whenever you shift away from the middle, you must recalculate your targets, since the hitting angles have been altered.

If you want to emulate the pros, you can stand near either side wall and then walk or back your way toward the middle before you actually hit the ball. This can build up a little momentum for your serve and help keep your opponent guessing as to what you're going to hit, but it's also going to tire you out a little faster if you're not in good playing shape. Besides, even after that fancy footwork, the pros still contact the ball very close to the center of the court.

Some club players like to stand off to one side in the service zone, thinking this will give them a better angle to hit an outright ace, or to force a weak return. But this is a myth. Instead of gaining any advantage, they limit the number of serves they can actually hit (3 or 4 instead of the 8 options they have in the middle), they expose the ball's direction to their opponent the instant it leaves the racquet, they open up a large part of the court for their opponent to hit into, and they are a greater distance from their proper coverage position.

RELOCATION AFTER THE SERVE

You can never be too fast in getting *out of the service zone and back into your relocation position,* slightly facing your opponent as he hits his return. By moving directly into position, 3 to 5 feet behind the back service line, you avoid two common problems among beginners and intermediates:

1. When you remain in the service zone, you're in an excellent position to cover your opponent's kill attempts that come out too high, but you otherwise leave yourself much too vulnerable to a smart opponent. Instead of gambling with kill attempts, your opponent will know that when you're up that close to the front wall, any good passing shot angled

In this sequence of the low-drive serve, the solid lines indicate where each player will move. In the first photo, the server hits and completely finishes her swing. Then she uses shuffle steps to relocate to her proper coverage position. In the third photo, she watches her opponent hit the ball and tries to anticipate the direction of his shot.

2

3

down-the-wall or cross-court, 2 to 3 feet high, will easily go by you. And even a hard blast right to where you are standing can easily jam you by arriving in the air or close to your feet.

2. If you run a little circle pattern away from where you actually want to relocate—which is actually in the heart of center court—then you open up the entire front wall to your opponent and thus nullify perfectly good serves. Running *away* from your center-court position is a natural tendency at first; either you're afraid of getting hit by your opponent's return if you remain in the middle of the court, or you think you have to give your opponent more freedom to shoot than he or she is actually entitled to. But remember: you can relocate properly in center court and still give your opponent open hitting lanes without endangering your body.

ANTICIPATING YOUR OPPONENT'S RETURN

The better player you become, the more you will meet opponents who can return even your good serves consistently—and offensively. That will place even more importance on your ability to relocate properly and to anticipate your opponent's return. Yet don't worry about a dozen mythical options he or she might have. There really are only three or four.

Let's say you serve into your opponent's backhand corner and shuffle back into center-court control. A competent opponent realizes he or she has only four basic shots: a kill attempt into the left front corner, passing shots down-the-wall or cross-court, or a ceiling ball. And since good players will try to aim most of these returns at your backhand, you should be anticipating in that direction first. But if your opponent can't go down-the-wall with his or her backhand, but can rip the ball cross-court, then you should move your relocation position slightly to the right side of the court.

Meanwhile, you're reminding yourself that if any error is made, the ball very likely is going to come to you in center court, and that if it arrives at waist level or below, you're going to make every attempt to cut it off, in the air or on one bounce. You have such a decisive positioning edge on your opponent that a 2-foot-high passing shot down the nearest side wall can easily go for a winner.

When your opponent hits a successful ceiling-ball return, then your best option is to hit a ceiling shot of your own. (See page 112, The Ceiling-Ball Rally.)

STAYING ALIVE WHEN YOUR SERVE GOES OFF-TARGET

Much as you might strive for precision, the racquetball court can be an unforgiving chamber when you achieve only near-precision. On the low-drive serve, for example, if you hit 12 inches to the left of your front-wall target, the ball will strike the side wall a little beyond the back service line and rebound out *behind* center court, in the middle of the court. Instead of locating the ball into the back left corner, your 12-*inch* error has magnified into a 8-*foot* blunder. Whenever your serve heads into that area behind center court and between the back corners, your first realization should be that you're in deep trouble. You don't have to run to a side wall, but you have to move far enough out of center court to allow your opponent to hit straight into the front wall. This opens up about two-thirds of the court and gives your opponent offensive hitting lanes, down which he or she should attempt either a low drive into the open court area or a pinch into the same front corner.

1

When you hit the ball into that area *behind* center court and between the back corners (as the server has done here with a misdirected low-drive serve), you must move off to the side to give your opponent an open hitting lane into the front wall. The photos here show the two best shots for the service returner: a down-the-wall pass, and a pinch shot into the left corner.

2

3

STRATEGY WITH YOUR SERVE

Never serve merely to be serving. When you step into the service zone, you have 10 seconds in which to hit the ball, so use this time not only to catch your breath, but to *visualize where you want to hit the front wall.* Focusing on a specific target, instead of a general area such as "low on the front wall," will sharpen your accuracy. In the back of your mind, you also want to have two primary purposes when you serve:

1. Always try to force a weak return by angling the ball into the back corners. Many players tend to start worrying about the nearness of the two walls and the fullness of their backswing instead of simply concentrating on the ball.

2. Hold on to your center-court position by keeping your serves out of the middle of that deep court area.

Meanwhile, as the match progresses, you'll try to determine your opponent's strengths and weaknesses. With experience, and an observant eye, you'll learn to sense what type of serves are most effective against players with certain playing styles and competitive temperaments.

• If you meet a "blaster" who likes to contact the ball around knee level, try to bring the ball up around shoulder level with medium-speed "Z's" or half-lobs. Keep mixing up the pace so he can't get in a groove.

• If your opponent likes to play a slower-paced game, introduce low drives and hard-hit "Z's" so you can get an aggressive style of play going. Force him to adapt to your game.

• When your opponent goes to the ceiling with every return, keep serving low drives and "Z's" that allow him minimal time to set up. This makes it harder for him to go to the ceiling effectively. And when he hits this return weakly, go for a kill attempt or a passing shot that keeps the pressure on; let him know he'll have to pay for his mistakes.

A related element of strategy here is that you always want to keep a variety of serves going so that your opponent never really knows what to expect. When you become too predictable and too patterned (*i.e.*, low drives on the first serve, "Z's" on the second, and always toward the same back corner), you give your opponent an edge in anticipation that can prove crucial. Against a good opponent, you're much easier to play. Visualize yourself as a baseball pitcher with 8 pitches at your command, and even if you only mix up 5 of them during a particular match, you will still keep your opponent guessing. The only time you want to keep going into one corner with one or two basic serves is when your opponent has such a glaring weakness on that side that he can't even get the ball back. But then the question is, if it's not tournament play: What's the fun in serving like that, for either player?

The server is guilty here of a screen serve. Her shot has hit the front wall and has traveled all the way back to the service zone before the returnee can see it. If this screen serve is good, then the server must hit again; if it goes for a fault, then it remains a fault.

CHARACTERISTICS
OF GOOD SERVING

To develop a winning serve, keep in mind these key points:

1. Stand so you can contact the ball in the *middle* of the service zone.

2. Learn the proper front-wall targets through practice and experimentation. This builds a solid foundation, and experience will then take over.

3. Force is not as important as accuracy, but you always want to work on increasing your velocity. When you serve without much steam on the ball—even with good direction—you give your opponent more time to set up. This is beneficial to the opponent who lacks a sound, fundamental swing, and whose weaknesses and idiosyncrasies are exploited by a hard-paced serve.

4. Relocate quickly back in center court, watching the ball and your opponent as you move. Set up properly in a good ready position, anticipating your opponent's return.

5. Never watch the front wall as you await the return or you will lose far too much reaction time.

6. When you relocate properly, your opponent has to be more accurate; he or she has to hit around you. But when your serve comes into that 13- to 14-foot area between the back corners, and within 4 or 5 feet of the back wall, you have to move aside—thus opening up some gaping hitting lanes.

7. If you're striving for perfection, then try not to have *any* serve bounce off the back wall. Any ball that comes off the back wall far enough for your opponent to set up will give your opponent an offensive return.

8. Understand that the day will come when hitting a good serve into the back corners will not automatically put your opponent on the defensive. That means your serve will simply have to have even more exact direction with hopefully more velocity. You will also realize that you need more than a good serve to maintain your serve. You have to go beyond that with good relocating, positioning, and anticipation.

PRACTICING THE SERVE

Learning to hit the front-wall targets shown in this chapter is the single most important aspect of the serve. Yet this doesn't ask you to do the impossible, or to strive for something only advanced players can ever really achieve. These targets are all laid out for you, and you can virtually master them all by yourself on an empty court if you have some black tape, two or three balls, a grasp of the basics, and a willingness to concentrate. In fact, serving is the easiest part of the game to practice, and the most enjoyable.

When you go to practice, the tape will enable you to place "X's" on the front wall for your respective targets, though you'll need a ladder for the high lob. Then stand just to one side of the middle of the service zone and concentrate not only on hitting as close to those targets as possible, but on relocating properly, with one or two little shuffle steps. Practice this total movement—the serve and relocation—so that it becomes ingrained as a unit.

You can study where your serve locates as you turn to watch your imaginary opponent. In fact, not having an opponent's return to worry about will enable you to concentrate solely on the serve, and where each serve actually travels. Is that low drive just skimming past the short line and dying back in the corner? Is your "Z" angling deep into the opposite back corner? Are your lobs staying off the back wall on the second bounce? Where do your serves go when you miss the target by 2 or 3 feet?

Don't get discouraged as you work on mastering these targets. This is a game of fixed angles and trajectories, and if you can eventually learn to hit your target 100 times in a row, the ball will carry into a back corner 100 times in a row. But it all starts on an empty practice court.

CHAPTER 9
THE
SERVICE
RETURN

If you can get a good swing into the ball and generate some velocity on your service return, then *go for a kill or a passing shot, down-the-wall or cross-court*. If you don't have this confidence, or the serve has simply put you too much on the defensive, then *go to the ceiling* and try to draw your opponent into the back of the court.

Three or four years ago, when the ball was a little slower and good play was very much dependent on endurance, the ceiling return was automatic unless you were absolutely sure you could kill the ball. But the better players today are much more aggressive; their first instinct is to take the offensive against any serve that isn't perfectly hit. They know that this is their best opportunity to win the service back immediately, and that a ceiling ball only preserves the status quo and can lead into a long, tough rally.

When you impress upon your opponent that you're going to jump on his weak or inaccurate serves—even if you only drive the ball straight at him in center court—then this extra mental pressure can cause him to error even more as he tries to ''aim'' the ball back into the corners, instead of blasting away naturally.

THE LOW-DRIVE SERVICE RETURN

In this sequence, the player awaits the serve with his weight evenly distributed and his racquet held around his knees to facilitate a rapid swing against low-drive serves. He is holding a backhand grip, since most serves will go to the backhand side. As he moves into the back corner to retrieve the ball, he carries his racquet around waist level. The racquet can then be easily drawn up into a cocked position when he gets into a hitting position.

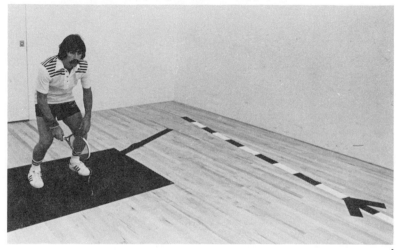

1

2

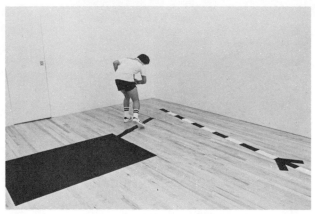

Going for the Ball

You want to stand behind the server, two steps off the back wall and midway between the side walls, with your knees bent slightly so you're ready to thrust quickly to either corner. Hold a backhand grip, with the racquet face between knee and thigh level. Concentrate completely on the ball as it travels into the front wall, and try to move instinctively to where you feel it will rebound. Don't lose valuable split-seconds by "freezing" in your ready position or debating with yourself; make up your mind and get your feet moving.

As you move toward the ball, bring the racquet up to around chest level so that it can be instantly pulled back into a cocked ready position as you set up for your shot. Then, by also staying low as you approach the ball, you're ready to react with a good swing if the ball suddenly "freaks" off the side wall, or rebounds crazily off both walls in the back corner.

OFFENSIVE RETURNS

When your opponent's serve gives you an offensive opportunity, don't let it slip away by taking a tentative, go-to-the-ceiling approach. Instead, when you reach the ball in time to set up, try one of the following shots:

● Drive the ball into the nearest front corner, either with *a kill attempt or a down-the-wall passing shot*. This is the shortest route to the front wall, and thus the quickest way to force your opponent out of center court. But remember, if you can't threaten your opponent with passing shots that stay off the side wall, then he or she will simply "cheat" toward the opposite side of the court in relocating after the serve.

● Probably the safest offensive return is the *cross-court passing shot*, since you have more of the court to hit into after the ball comes off the front wall. Aim this shot directly into the middle of the front wall, with enough force to drive the ball past your opponent, who's in center court. If you miss, try to error on the near side of the front wall (the side of the court from which you are hitting), as low as possible, so the ball will be blasted directly at your opponent without rebounding off a side wall. This gives your opponent less time to react and a tougher shot to deal with.

● When the serve comes into that area *behind* center court, and the server moves off to the side, you have two-thirds of an open court with which to end the point. Don't get fancy: just go for a safe passing shot down-the-wall, 2 to 3 feet high, or a pinch shot into the front corner on the open side of the court.

Here are the two sound offensive options on the service return: the down-the-wall drive for a kill or a pass, and the cross-court pass. The ceiling ball is the best defensive return and would take the same path as the down-the-wall pass, except that it's hit up to the ceiling.

• Any time your opponent's serve bounces off the back wall and gives you enough room to set up, you've received a gift. So move quickly into position and drive the ball offensively into the front wall.

• When your opponent serves a half-lob that you can't cut off in the air, or that doesn't come off the back wall, then your best return is a ceiling. But that gets into a pretty slow pattern of play, and you may have already lost a couple of rallies going that route. So occasionally you may want to drive the ball cross-court or hit a ''Z'' shot into the opposite front corner, which should force your opponent into the deep part of the court while you move into center court. This may still give your opponent a good shot, but it will be from deep court, where your opponent should be less effective. Lob serves are difficult to kill on the fly because you're contacting a ball angling down, about 35 feet from the front wall. (The "Z" serve is traveling too fast and on too sharp an angle to enable you to cut it off in the air before it hits the floor.)

THE CEILING RETURN

Much as you might want to take an offensive approach to this game, certain opponents are simply going to force you onto the defensive with an assortment of accurately placed serves. The ceiling shot is your best option in these situations. It allows you some margin for error and, when properly hit, will drive your opponent back alongside you in deep court—thus evening up the rally. (When you go to the ceiling, remember that your target area is about 2 to 3 feet before the front wall, and that you want to direct the ball toward your opponent's backhand corner.)

However, if you're hitting ceiling returns during the entire match against a person on your own ability level, then very likely you're taking an overly defensive approach to this game. You're using your return to simply get a foothold in the rally—to start things off even—instead of trying to gain initial control with a more aggressive approach.

TIPS FOR GOOD RETURNS

1. Always think in terms of overall center-court strategy. You want your offensive returns to push your opponent forward or to the sides, and you want your ceiling balls to force him back.
2. You want to be the aggressor whenever possible, but with the

understanding that unreasonable—or poorly executed—offensive shots will give your opponent easy put-aways.

3. However, don't be inhibited by thinking that just because you miss an offensive return, your opponent is going to kill it every time. He may not be ready, or able, to capitalize on all of his scoring opportunities.

4. Since your opponent controls center court, it's crucial that your offensive shots *hit the front wall first* (except on tight pinches), and low enough so they don't bounce off the back wall. Even if they come back to him forcefully in the middle of the court, it's better than giving your opponent a slow-moving "plum" in front court.

5. If your opponent is serving weakly, keep blasting away and get the match over with (in tournament competition). But against a competent opponent, try to mix up your returns so that he or she is always in a quandary, not knowing what to anticipate.

6. Good returns boil down to the basics. Quick reactions and the right instincts will be wasted if you lack a full-shoulder backhand swing or a wrist-snapping forehand motion. When you try to flick at the ball and hope for the best, you do a lot of hoping.

7. Strive to always get your racquet back quickly, in its cocked ready position, as you wait for the ball to come off the side or back wall. Even the pros have trouble with a ball that "freaks" off a wall or suddenly jumps toward them, but they still make the play because their racquet is always ready.

8. If your opponent serves so hard or so well that you can barely dig the ball out in the back corners, don't give up. Do everything you can to flick the ball to the front wall so that at least it stays in play. Then you'll always have a chance that your opponent might miss your "plum." If that happens, you're lucky—but it's nice to combine some retrieving skill with some luck.

CHAPTER 10
MATCH PLAY TACTICS

Now that I've armed you with the center-court strategy and with the shots you need to make this system work, the following chapter should help you pull everything together when you play a match.

HITTING THE RIGHT SHOT AT THE RIGHT TIME

Good players try to be creative in their overall shot selection during a match; they want to keep their attack diversified so that their opponent cannot easily anticipate where the ball is going. But in doing so, they should never lose sight of their center-court strategy, which helps them take the correct percentage shot. Following are the ways you can narrow down your own options and decide objectively what shot to hit from different locations on the court. Let your opponent do all the gambling when it comes to shot-making.

When you're hitting a backhand from 25 feet away and your opponent is properly located, your best offensive opportunities are: (1) a kill attempt straight into the left corner and (2) a cross-court pass to the right. If your kill attempt is hit too high, it may still run down the left wall for a successful pass.

1. Learn Your Scoring Range

You want to play this game as offensively as possible, but only when you know your scoring potential with each stroke at varying distances from the front wall. For example, when you are 25 feet away, are you capable of pinching the ball for a winner? Killing the ball straight in? Going down-the-wall for a pass? How is your accuracy affected when you move back to 30 feet? Do your pinches start popping into the middle of the court? Do your passing shots carom off the side wall, or rebound off the back wall as "plums" because you're hitting the ball too high? Is this true on your backhand, but not on your forehand until you get back to about 35 feet? How is your accuracy affected by the amount of time you have to set up properly?

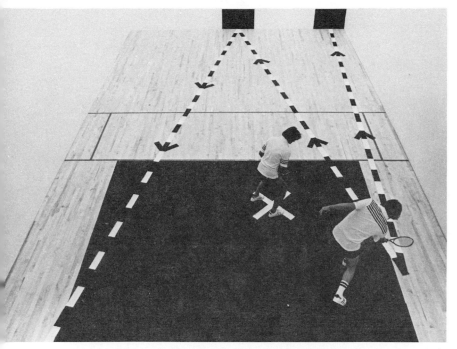

From the right side of the court, 30 feet away, with your opponent properly located, try for a kill into the right corner, but, again, realize that a down-the-wall passing shot may result. Mix in cross-court passes to push your opponent into his or her backhand corner.

In determining your scoring range, keep in mind that your shot-selection strategy is the same on both sides of the court and from center-court, as well: drive the ball into the nearest front corner for a kill attempt or a down-the-wall passing shot that dies in the back corner. If you don't have this ability, go for the cross-court pass, and then the ceiling ball—in that order. There's not much else you can do if you want to play *good* racquetball. You don't want to bring the ball into the middle, and this is what you risk with specialty shots like the diagonal kill attempt, the around-the-wall-ball, the overhead, and the "Z" ball.

Through practice and experience, your goal will be to keep moving your scoring range farther away from the front wall.

2. Diversify Your Attack

When you can mix up your kill attempts and passes on both sides of the court, you gain two advantages.

First, your opponent can't predict your shot. Instead of "cheating" to one side of the court or the other, he must locate himself in the middle in order to cover your down-the-wall or cross-court passes, and this leaves him vulnerable to accurate shots to either side.

Second, you keep your opponent moving. By hitting the right shot—as offensively as possible—even your misses can force him wide or into the back corners.

3. Think Offensively

You must learn to sense scoring opportunities and try to capitalize on them. When you pass up an offensive opportunity inside your scoring range (by jamming the ball up into the ceiling, *etc.*), you give your opponent a reprieve and time to set up for his next shot. Prolonging the rally may even give him that same opportunity you passed up—only he goes for it, and scores.

Conversely, when you take the right shot and miss it a little, the velocity of the ball will many times keep your opponent from killing it, and so you haven't really lost anything; you're still in or near center court, but, more importantly, you took a scoring situation and you tried to score—you had a chance at winning the rally. That's offensive racquetball.

That's why the pinch shot is a weapon you must employ in certain situations. You hit this shot knowing that if the ball hits on too wide an angle into either wall, or is hit too high, then it's going to come right back to your opponent for a "plum." But the pinch is one of your "must" scoring shots, and you can't avoid it. Let's say you're shooting from around 28 feet on the right side and your opponent is slightly to your left, in center court. There's no better shot from here than the pinch shot— *when it's hit low* —and you should learn to go for it, even though it has that inherent flaw, should you miss. You can't constantly shoot up and down the side wall or go cross-court, because a competent opponent knows that both of these types of shots tend to land deep in the court, and then he can simply lag back a little on you. The pinch shot will keep him honest and force him to move forward. Furthermore, along the way you have to go for *winners* in this game, and accept whatever happens. So practice the pinch and learn to score with it.

Hitting the ball into alleys 1 and 3 will produce good passing shots away from your opponent.

Hitting into alleys 2 and 4 will funnel balls right to your opponent. If you're going to error, it's better to hit alley 2 with good velocity because your opponent will have to execute a good reflex shot in order to score from his center-court position. Alley 4 represents what we term a diagonal kill attempt. It should be avoided. Not only do you risk hitting your opponent with the ball, but the slightest error will kick your shot into the middle of the court.

4. Keep the Pressure on Your Opponent

You apply pressure on your opponent by having good center-court positioning—but you tighten the screws by letting your opponent know that you're always going to try to score from here, and that you're not going to let him off the hook by playing the ball defensively.

Here's the thinking you want to convey: "Okay, I'm going to cover the middle, and I'm going to be waiting for all of your mistakes. I'm even going to be able to cover most of your good shots. Now the pressure's on you: *hit your shot*. And you'd better be precise."

That's the best psych job you can lay on your opponent. When he knows you're studying his swing and anticipating his shot, then it's tough for him to execute properly. He knows if he errors, you're going to be waiting to rip the ball low into the front wall. This forces him to hit the ball as accurately as possible, and many times the added pressure results in even more errors. Even if you fail to hit outright winners, the ball will come to your opponent low and hard, and you will either drive him off to one side to make a play or force him to execute a good "reflex" stroke in center court.

Good, constant velocity on your shots is also going to exploit an opponent with a fundamentally unsound swing. If your opponent has obvious flaws in his swing, don't give him time to get his weird little motion in gear, because he probably has it grooved pretty well. Instead, keep driving the ball hard off the front wall and often he'll get caught in the middle of his swing when the ball arrives.

5. Other Hitting Situations

● If you're on the run and can barely get to the ball, and your choice is between the ceiling ball, the "Z" ball, and the around-the-wall-ball, then jam the ball up into the ceiling toward your opponent's backhand. You really won't have time to aim this shot properly, but by hitting it hard up into the ceiling you at least drive your opponent out of center court with a ball that caroms perhaps 33 or 35 feet deep, while you hustle into the middle to cover.

● Although I place a lot of emphasis on hitting the front wall first when you drive the ball, there are times when you want to use the side wall going into the front wall. This is especially true when your opponent is out of position in deep court, or is always lagging back too far. If you keep blasting the ball, then all of your velocity shots that are hit too high are going to bounce right to him. But when you can pinch the ball tight, or hit farther back on the side wall with a ball that is still kept low, then you will force your opponent to thrust forward to retrieve it.

SCORING FROM CENTER COURT

These photos show five different scoring opportunities from the heart of center court. When the hitter's opponent is on her left side, her best options are:

1

Kill the ball straight into the front wall.

Pass the ball up and down the right wall.

Pinch the ball tight into the right corner.

When the hitter's opponent is on her right side, she can:

Hit a cross-court pass down the left side of the court.

Pinch the ball tight into the front right corner.

FUNDAMENTALS OF GOOD PLAY

● Get warmed up properly. Have your body stretched out so there are minimal chances of muscle pulls and you feel confident about going after balls in the first rally.

● Be prepared—mentally—to play your match. If many different ideas or outside worries are on your mind during an important match, then you must evaluate your concentration powers.

● If you've never played your opponent before, then on your first couple of serves hit low drives into his backhand corner. Find out immediately if he can execute the stroke properly. He might get lucky the first or second time, but there's no hiding a weak backhand against persistent low-drive serves.

● When serving, concentrate on hitting those front-wall targets so that you keep your opponent pinned in the back corners. Then relocate properly so that your opponent must execute pinpoint returns.

● On your service return, take the offensive against your opponent's weaker serves, but learn to adjust and go to the ceiling if you are giving up too many easy points by being overly aggressive.

● Once the rally begins, vary your shots to avoid becoming too predictable. But stick to sound, fundamental shots that are dictated not by sudden whims, but by center-court strategy and your position on the court in relation to your opponent.

● Try to score from within your scoring range with kill-shot attempts, or with passing shots away from your opponent. Then position yourself in center court so that your opponent is forced to hit these same shots.

● Be aggressive in gaining, maintaining, and regaining center court. Don't let yourself be easily driven away.

● You are going to miss far more shots than you hit for outright winners, so strive to hit the kinds of shots that will still give your opponent trouble, even as errors.

● Don't exaggerate the angles you need to hit on the front wall for low-drive serves and cross-court passes. The tendency is to hit too far to one side, instead of concentrating on target areas near the middle of the wall.

● Try to make solid racquet contact with the ball. This will give you maximum velocity on all your shots.

● Keep your eyes on the ball as you are taking your stroke—and as your opponent is hitting.

● Don't let your mind go lax. Good anticipation should be a continuous part of your game.

• When you are under stress, stick to the fundamentals. But be aggressive. Don't opt for lesser shots that add very little to your game.

• Don't worry about learning psyching techniques to use against your opponent. If he likes to wage psychological warfare, just let him know early in the match that you're going to try to beat him with a solid, emotionless game; go after him with basic shots and see how he reacts. That's how Davey Bledsoe defeated Marty Hogan in the finals of the 1977 Nationals. Hogan was hitting good shots—but Bledsoe kept hitting better ones. Eventually this pressure got too great for Hogan.

• Try to maintain your own game style—the one you're comfortable with—rather than get caught up in your opponent's game style. If you're always playing off your opponent, then he can easily convert you to his style of play by simply being aggressive or slowing down the action. Then you're at his mercy.

For example, let's say you prefer a driving, attacking type of game, and you meet a more deliberate soft-hitter. If you're not careful, he'll get you into ceiling-ball rallies that are out of your element, but in which he's quite confident; you may get so frustrated after 10 minutes that you end up losing when you should have won.

To counteract this player's strategy, you must stick with your game plan by hitting the ball with velocity whenever possible and creating the action when you can. If he tries to start ceiling-ball rallies, respond with overhead drives when the time is appropriate. Try to serve so low and hard that he can't go to the ceiling with his return. On all of your shots, try to force him into quick actions, quick movements, and quick decisions so that he doesn't have a chance to play deliberately. When he serves half-lobs and high lobs, try to cut the ball off by volleying it in the air before it gets into the back corner—then drive the ball down-the-wall or cross-court. This forces him to react quickly, and he doesn't feel comfortable playing that way. Instead, he wants you to let his lob serves get into the back corners, where they are difficult to return offensively, and which thus force a defensive pace.

• Strive to keep the ball out of center court.

• Play hard.

PREPARING FOR A TOURNAMENT

If you're entered in a Friday-to-Sunday tournament, and you are accustomed to playing three or four times a week, here's a program you might want to follow in the four days leading up to your first match.

Monday: Play a hard match. Hit all your shots and your serves, go after every ball, dive when you have to, and don't even be thinking about a tournament. Just work on playing correct racquetball. If you're running on the side, continue your regular schedule today and Tuesday, but don't increase your mileage.

Tuesday: Play another tough match. Really get your mind into the game and push yourself to hustle and play hard. When you get home, make sure your equipment is in ready order. Do you have enough gloves and wristbands? Does your racquet need a new handle? Don't wait to check until Thursday night and then get all nervous when you go to the club Friday and find out they don't have any rubber grips. If you have two racquets, check your spare, as well.

Wednesday: Start resting your body for the tournament. Try to ease off and not even play. You may have 3 days of hard matches coming up over the weekend. If you're so antsy that you've just got to do *something* on the court, then hit balls for 15 or 20 minutes, but don't play anybody because you're going to start to think you're already playing a match in the tournament. Save that *intensity*. Your muscles are probably tight from Monday and Tuesday, so stretch them out good, maybe twice during the day. If you wait until right before your first match on Friday, your muscles will have tightened up so much that stretching could take a lot out of you.

Thursday: REST. Put your racquet in the closet. There's nothing you can do on the practice court today that will help you win on Friday. Get off your feet, go to a movie, or do whatever is enjoyable and relaxing. Many people spend too many hours on Wednesday and Thursday playing the tournament in their mind. They've already played the finals and collected their first-place trophy. This only drains them, and sometimes it makes it hard to get fired up for the actual matches. If you love to play racquetball, your body will sense that you have important matches on the weekend, and it will be ready without having to hype it up.

Friday: I recommend eating a balanced meal at least 3½ hours before a tough match. Let your digestive system complete its cycle. You'll find that you play better when you're a little hungry. Give your body a complete stretch before your match so that you are ready to play hard on the very first point. From the two days of not playing, your body should be raring to go. I'm sure you'll be nervous when you start to play, and you may be worried: "Have I lost my kill shot?" Relax. In two days you haven't lost anything. In fact, you've built up more of a desire to play. After a few rallies you'll be loosened up nicely. In the tournament itself, concentrate. It will get you a long way when you're playing under pressure.

CHAPTER 11

IMPROVING YOUR GAME

Once you get involved in competitive racquetball, you will want to know ways to improve your game so you can win your share of matches against the people you play regularly. You may even have your sights set on a neighbor, a business associate, or a friendly scoundrel at your club whom you'd love to beat. This chapter, therefore, will help you take what you've learned in this book and apply it toward your self-improvement. You can achieve higher ability levels not only through a little *physical education*—by taking time to practice your strokes and to improve your conditioning—but through *mental analysis* of your opponents' style of play, and your own strengths and weaknesses.

SCOUTING YOUR OPPONENTS

When you're playing the same basic opponents week after week, you're already going to know quite a bit about their approach to the game. But you can greatly increase this knowledge by ''scouting'' them from the gallery as they play a match. You'll find that you can be much more observant about flaws in their strategy and shot selection when you're a spectator, and you can gain some fresh insights by noticing how other people play your rivals. This will help you plot your own strategy for future matches.

In scouting like this, be a little discreet. Racquetball is still at the point where your friends may get a little hostile if they see you taking notes as they play. They may think: "Hey, you're getting pretty technical, buddy. We're out here for fun." So, instead, just pick out two or three things to study in your mind, and evaluate them closely. For example:

• What type of serve does he like to use? Does he try to hit everything into the backhand corner? How well does he keep the ball from rebounding off the back wall?

• After serving, does he stay in the service zone—making him vulnerable to cross-court passes—or does he locate properly in center court, which means you're going to have to hit accurate shots around him?

• On his service returns, does he try to go into the nearest front corner or down the side wall whenever possible? *Can* he go into that corner when the ball comes to his backhand, or must he go cross-court? Is he much more offensive with his forehand?

• When he goes cross-court with his shots, does he hit the proper front-wall angle, or does the ball consistently rebound off the side walls into the middle, or carom off the back wall?

• Does he have a particular weakness on either stroke—the backhand or forehand—that will allow you to "cheat" to the left or right side of the court, or to hang back deeper than usual? If he can't kill his backhand into the left corner, then you'll know you can move over to the right side until he proves that he can hit the ball up and down the left wall.

• What does he do with his set-up shots? Example: the ball comes to him on the right side at about 30 feet and his opponent is properly positioned in the middle. Does he kill into the right corner? Go cross-court? Or does he shoot a lesser shot such as a diagonal into the left corner, a "Z" ball, an around-the-wall-ball, or a ceiling ball?

• How aggressive is he in center court? Does he seem anxious to volley, and, if so, how effective is he? Can he get his racquet set quickly and hit with reasonable power and accuracy from an open-stance position?

• How does he play the side walls, and balls off the back wall, and where does he tend to shoot these shots?

• Check his tempo of play. Everybody has a dominant tempo: fast-paced, medium, slow. They may try to play a different pace once in a while, but there are very few players who can switch successfully during the course of a match between playing fast and then slowing it down.

• Does he have an effective ceiling-ball game, and does he like to play that general style? When the rally gets into an aggressive situation where it's hit-hit-hit, does he shy away by going to the ceiling and slowing down the rally again?

• Notice his overall pattern of court coverage. Where does he like to position himself during a rally? How quickly does he react? Can he stretch out for balls and maintain good balance?

Detailed questioning like this is going to help you immensely the next time you play an opponent you have scouted. You're going to be more aware of weaknesses you can exploit and strengths you should try to neutralize, and you'll find yourself playing with better anticipation and more confidence. Still, you must follow up your critique by trying to be a little more observant as you play. Try to notice two or three of the items from the previous checklist and then afterward review your match on paper, while everything is fresh—your opponent's game, as well as your own. After a couple of matches, you'll notice definite patterns emerging in both your playing styles, and this will make your game plan even more realistic and effective in the future.

This approach to scouting can, of course, be used for when you want to size up a couple of new members in the club, or before you play a ''challenge'' match on your club ladder, or during a local tournament when you have a chance to watch your prospective opponents play a match. You can learn a lot by watching a player when you have specifics in mind, but realize that you obviously can't get the feel of playing him until you're actually in a match together. That's when you'll be able to evaluate such things as: (1) his pace on the ball; (2) how well he can return the ball; (3) how quick he is in covering the court; (4) exactly how far he can stretch and get to balls. It's crucial to pick these things out as early as possible so that you can make any necessary adjustments.

ANALYZING YOUR OWN GAME

Scouting your opponents will be meaningless unless you also develop an *objective* understanding of your own strengths and weaknesses. Only then can you compare abilities with the people you play and devise a realistic game plan that will hopefully lead to victory.

In trying to analyze what you can actually do out on the court, take the approach that you're an opponent and you've set out to beat yourself. Study the previous scouting checklist and see how your own game fares. We all think we can perform better than we actually do, so if the comparison between you and your opponent is to work, then your own ego must be stripped out of the evaluation. (There will be time enough to gloat later, if you do your homework honestly now.) For example, you must be able to dispassionately judge your speed against your opponent: Can you run him to exhaustion? Do you even have the shots to try?

Or, how does your backhand compare with his backhand? Can he be overpowered on the left side? Or does he take your down-the-wall attempts to his backhand and kill them or hit low cross-court drives?

Try to think about where your shots have been locating. How many of them are coming off the back wall as "plums" for your opponent? Are your passing shots actually ending up in the back corners when they get past your opponent? Or are they caroming off the side walls into the middle?

As humble as you want to be in this self-analysis, don't analyze and revise your game plan so much that you are in constant flux, never settling on a style of play that fits your competitive nature. You want to have the confidence that you can think through your strokes and your strategy and then say, "Okay, I'm going to approach the game this way. And I'm going to give it the full test. I'm going to let my system operate under pressure, on good days and bad days. And then after eight or ten matches, I'll be able to make some sound judgments."

Yet along the way, be wise enough to accept the fallacies of your own analysis—and a breakdown of your strokes. It's not just a matter of determining why your own shots aren't working, but also admitting that your opponent probably has something to do with your frustration. Maybe he's better than you gave him credit for.

Practicing Alone

Try to practice by yourself when you're working to groove the proper forehand and backhand strokes. Then you're not distracted or worried about an opponent on the court, and you can concentrate on your swing. Just hit the ball slowly to yourself off the front wall so you have plenty of time to get into position, set your racquet, and hit into the ball.

If you're working on a variety of shots, move about the court to keep your practice interesting. For example, you might start out near the back wall and hit ceiling shots until you make an error—then pounce on that mistake and either kill it or drive it cross-court. Try to visualize your opponent in center court as you hit.

After that, move into the service zone and try to direct all your low-drive and "Z" serves into the back corners. Remember to snap your wrist and get that good velocity. When you practice the lob serves, remember to tighten up your wrist slightly so you can get exact direction.

You also don't need an opponent to practice pinching the ball into the front corners and "reading" how the ball comes out. Simply hit all your different-angled pinch shots using the front wall and side walls, and then try to kill the balls that rebound back high to you.

Good strokes take time to develop, so be patient. Practicing alone, or even with a friend, may not be very exciting—but it's productive. And as your shots improve in practice, they will become much more automatic when you get into competition.

PRACTICING YOUR STROKES

Playing regularly is going to improve your game simply by giving you a better sense of shot selection and court coverage. But only by practicing on an empty court—alone or with a friend—will you be able to groove accurate strokes that can be trusted in the heat of a match. Practice is also necessary if what you're striving for up the road is to defeat people who are beating you consistently right now.

You don't have to spend an entire hour practicing; a 30-minute session once or twice a week will be more than what most C and B players devote to practicing. In fact, everybody is so let's-play-a-game conscious that it's hard to find a person who just wants to work on specific strokes. Fortunately, however, this is a game that you can practice effectively by yourself.

Practicing with a Friend

When you find a good practice partner, only your imagination can hold you back when it comes to devising drills that will sharpen your strokes and your court-coverage ability. Some suggestions:

1. Have one person work on serves while his opponent practices service returns. When the person is tired of serving, then reverse positions. You can even go beyond this and practice the third shot of the rally by having the server relocate and then try to kill or pass his opponent's service return. Play out the entire rally if you need competition to spur your concentration, but avoid keeping track of the points to see who's "winning." The idea is to work on your strokes, to experiment, to study what is happening to the ball. Try to keep your ego out of it.

2. You can set up specific scoring situations we discussed in the book, such as having one person shooting from 25 to 30 feet along either side of the court while his opponent tries to make a play from his center-court position.

3. Both of you can practice your "reflex" shots from the front of center court by standing alongside each other in this area and then

banging the ball straight into the front wall. Each person attempts to kill or pass the ball. This is great practice for your reactions in responding to shots that are angling to you in the middle of the court. The ball is coming fast and you have to get your racquet set quickly so that you can execute properly.

4. Practice ceiling-ball rallies exactly as you would play them in a game.

Concentration

Racquetball is played in such a demanding environment—physically and mentally—that it's natural from time to time during a match to let yourself "tune out" when you feel your mind overloading with thoughts about technique, strategy, and position . . . and just plain exhaustion.

Here's a good drill to help you learn to *concentrate* on concentrating. In your next 60-minute match, try to determine your level of concentration as you are playing. Then critique yourself afterward to see what percentage of that hour you were focused on the game, and not your outside world. Take the same test for a few more matches and see if there's any improvement.

It's tough, I know, to keep thoughts of business or household pressures from interfering with on-court concentration. But if you're playing racquetball for relaxation—and also to win—then try to leave your work and your worries at the door. Don't lose sight of the fact that racquetball should be a fun game that completely absorbs your attention for the hour or so that you play. When you learn to appreciate this therapeutic value, then you gain the full enjoyment of what this game has to offer.

CONDITIONING

A lot of tennis players complain: "I played two sets of tennis and gained a pound." But you never find this happening after 45 minutes or an hour of racquetball. This is a game of few delays and continuous movement. Thus, you keep your heart beat up between points, and you sweat—which is great for your physical conditioning, but disastrous to your skills until you're in reasonably good shape. Even though your mind is willing, your body will be protesting after 10 or 15 minutes if you aren't prepared to cope with the prolonged effort and the fast action needed to play the game right. Your legs will get weary and you'll start playing standing straight up. So much for your shots, and your mobility.

If you don't feel confident about stretching out to reach for the ball—

because you're afraid you won't get back up—this inhibits your effectiveness in covering the court. Conversely, you'll expand your center-court coverage when your body is ready and willing to thrust to either side of the court with one cross-over step and a good stretch.

Following are ways you can improve your conditioning so that you can keep your body and mind in a state of alertness and eagerness as long as possible during the match. Attrition will very often decide your matches, so let your opponent be the one to call for an oxygen break.

1. The game itself is such an excellent conditioner that two or three sessions a week will lead to a flatter belly, a skinnier backside, and an overall feeling of "good muscle tone." It can keep a three-times-a-week player in pretty good shape, once he or she gets that way. But it's tough work trying to develop stamina and a forehand at the same time, so I like people to augment their conditioning in other ways.

2. Just plain running, on a regular basis, will help considerably by increasing your endurance. I like to run 2 to 3 miles a day along San Diego beaches. I also mix in some short sprints, which correlate with racquetball's explosiveness.

3. To improve your ability to thrust out for the ball, or to take one or two quick steps in any direction, try this exercise either before or after you run: do 3 standing long jumps in one direction, striving for good balance when you land. Then turn around and make 3 more jumps, trying to get back past your original starting position.

4. Find any open area (or use the court itself) and stand in center court, ready for an imaginary ball to come off the front wall toward the right or left back corner. Then respond with an explosive movement to that corner, get into a hitting position with your knees bent and the racquet set, and then execute a complete swing that emphasizes total body movement. When your swing is completed, explode back to the original starting position.

5. An excellent overall drill that will leave you winded after a 30-second burst is "shadow racquetball." Get on an empty court, in your backyard, or on beach sand and go through the basic court movements and strokes you use to control the center-court area. Hit a forehand from 30 feet, retreat into your backhand corner for a ceiling ball, hit a ceiling shot, and then move up to center court to cover your opponent's overhead drive. Stretch out for a backhand volley, move over and cut the ball off with your forehand, and then retreat again for a ceiling. This is a great exercise because you only need a 20-by-20-foot area, and you can work on your conditioning, good racquetball strokes, and quick movements simultaneously.

CHAPTER 12
DOUBLES

Doubles is a game that's growing in popularity as court space becomes limited in certain clubs and as more players learn the fundamentals of proper strategy and etiquette. There are a number of reasons for the game's appeal:

- There's the camaraderie of four people getting together and playing a match, with the joking and friendly competition that usually results.

- Since you have to protect only one side of the court, you don't need the conditioning that a full hour of singles would require.

- If you have trouble playing singles because of a feeble backhand, you can protect yourself by playing the right side of the court, where you can hit forehands nearly the entire match. All you need is a partner with a decent backhand to cover the left side.

- There's the challenge of having to execute your shots much more accurately than in singles, since you have two opponents covering the ball—on the same-sized court.

- The action in center court is usually faster than in singles, thus resulting in even more of a ''reflex'' game. This is good practice for the quick, open-stance swing you need in singles.

- Doubles is a thinking person's game. A team that can play together efficiently can often overcome and defeat a team that has brute strength or greater individual skills. A great singles player, in fact, can often be a terrible doubles player.

These virtues of the game, however, lead to one warning for beginners:

wait until you have a good grasp of singles before tackling doubles. The action is so fast, with four players swinging four racquets in such a small area, that the game can be absolutely confusing and even physically dangerous unless *all four players* know what they're doing. It takes just one person in the foursome who doesn't understand the basic movements and etiquette to cause a great deal of chaos.

ETIQUETTE

Just as in singles, respect for one another is mandatory if you want your rallies to run smoothly and result in fun play. If you're not prepared to give your opponents an unobstructed swing at the ball and their rightful shots, there should be a doctor on call.

In basic rally situations, each team must strive to give its opponents open hitting lanes for the following three shots: (a) a straight-in kill; (b) a pinch into the nearest front corner; (c) the proper cross-court angle.

The nature of doubles emphasizes the short, efficient swing that you have hopefully acquired in singles play. This swing is safer and much more effective in center-court exchanges, where three players are normally positioned close together. In deep court, however, there's usually enough room to take a full-body swing.

THE BASIC FORMATIONS

Side-by-Side

This is the most logical formation and the most efficient way to play doubles. Each player has basic responsibilities on his half of the court, with the understanding that whenever he gets out of position, his teammate will shift and cover his area.

True side-by-side is best executed when one player is left-handed and the other right-handed. This allows the team to cover the major passing and scoring lanes with crunching forehands. They then only have to decide who should cover shots down the middle, and that will obviously be the person with the stronger backhand.

Modified Side-by-Side

Since there are relatively few lefty-righty teams, the modified side-by-side formation will most often be used when two right-handers are teammates. The right-side player's major responsibility is to cover the

"I" Formation

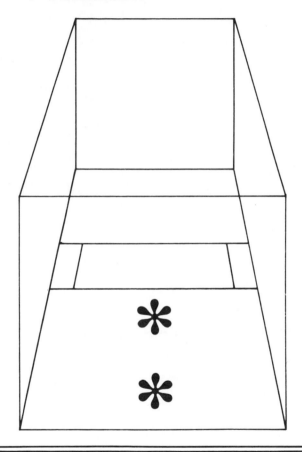

Modified Side-by-Side

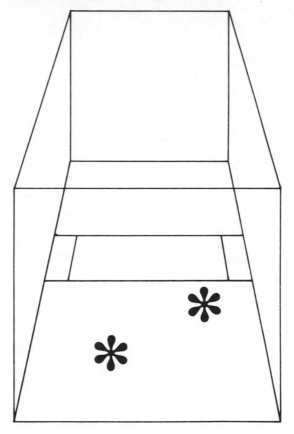

Side-by-Side

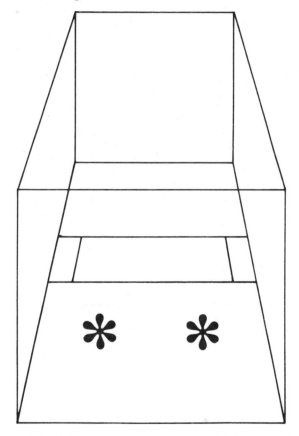

right front corner, where most points are scored. The player with the stronger backhand will hold down the left side.

This formation enables a team with two right-handers to account for the fact that the left side is being covered by a backhand, which rarely holds the same offensive potential as the forehand. Therefore, the left-side player generally lags a little deeper to protect his backhand. This sets up a diagonal coverage pattern and takes into consideration the strengths of both players.

The "I" Formation

This approach capitalizes on the specific assets of each member by having one player up and the other player back. The front player is quicker, has more aggressiveness in court coverage, and is a better retriever. The person in back shoots the ball better from deep court and has good control of his ceiling game.

Thus, each player has the maximum amount of room in which to operate and execute his skills. The retriever is in the center court alone, so he has a full range of potential kill opportunities. His teammate can float from side to side in deep court, covering well-placed passes and controlling the ceiling game.

The difficulty is in finding two players who have these qualities, and to then get them together as a doubles team.

THE BASIC SHOTS

The Serve

Proper serving is necessary to get good doubles started. Serve from the middle of the service zone and aim for the back corners, using the same front-wall targets as in singles. Accuracy on your serve is more important than power. But, again, remember: this is a game in which we'd like to master *both*.

Be careful not to serve low drives or half-lobs into the back corner behind your partner. The timing of your opponent's return down this side wall will usually result in welts on the back side of your teammate as he relocates. "Z" serves and high lobs into that back corner will take away this worry.

Team A-B is playing team C-D. Against a right-handed team, A will try to serve the ball into area 3, because that is D's backhand corner. By standing in the middle, the server has all the proper hitting angles to direct the ball to both back corners. Player B must stay in the service zone with his back to the wall until the served ball passes the back service line. Players C and D share the back court and are located 2 steps off the back wall.

If team C-D is a right-handed-left-handed combination (as in the photograph), the server should learn to angle the ball into alley 2, since that forces backhand returns from either opponent. A good server is thus one who can serve into alleys 1, 2, and 3 with diversification and accuracy. Since control of the serve is more important than force, the server may hit with three-quarters speed until good direction is consistently achieved.

The Serve Return

This is dependent on the success of your opponent's serve. If he serves weakly, make an aggressive return by attempting to kill the ball or drive it cross-court. It's advantageous to widen the angle on your cross-court pass so that it has a greater chance of going by your opponent. (Have it hit the side wall just behind where your opponent is standing.) You should also try to volley and drive any lob serves, since this will get you closer to the center-court position.

On excellent serves, go to the ceiling. If you try to hit an unreasonable offensive return, it may float up weakly to the front wall, where both your opponents will be ready to pounce on it.

The Pinch Shot

This is a game in which you have to kill the ball to score the majority of your points because you have opponents placed on both sides of the court to track down your passing shot.

The pinch shot is a particularly valuable scoring weapon, because you often find one of your opponents lagging back a bit, playing defensively, or looking for the cross-court pass. Pinching the ball into the open front-court area will thus be very effective. If this opponent starts to cheat too far forward to cover the pinch, then he's highly vulnerable to the wide-angled pass.

Through your doubles experience, you'll find that your opponent on the opposite side of the court can't cover both your cross-court pass and your side-wall, front-wall pinch. So mix these shots up and keep your opponents in a quandary.

If the serve goes to player D, let's examine the responsibilities of each player. D's options with his return are: (1) a kill attempt into the left corner that, if hit too high, can result in a successful passing shot down the left wall; (2) a cross-court pass by A; (3) a ceiling ball.

Player B's responsibilities (after relocating in a center-court position) are to cover the left-corner kill attempt or left-wall pass, or a ceiling-ball return into the back left corner.

A relocates after serving, turns to watch D hit the ball, and anticipates D's cross-court pass. A will also have to retreat and cover D's ceiling ball if he angles it into the deep right corner.

C moves up slightly behind A and B and is ready to cover their next shot. (One common myth of racquetball doubles is that one team plays completely up and the other team plays completely back. But as these photographs show, both teams are always jockeying for the best possible position. This means that one member of the team is always trying to be located in center court, or slightly behind. If both members of the team are deep together, they are going to lose.)

If D's return comes to B, then B's shot options are: (1) kill the ball into the left corner, which can also result in a pass down the left wall; (2) cross-court the ball past C.

Meanwhile, D has moved up after hitting so that he's ready to cover B's shot. C has also moved up to her team's right-side coverage position. A has given C this rightful position (C must be given room to hit B's cross-court pass attempt), but A will be ready to move in and cover C or D's next shot.

Notice how all team members are watching the ball so they all know what's going on.

If D's return goes to A, her shot options are: (1) kill the ball into the right corner or drive it down the right wall; (2) cross-court the ball by D.

Note that D has moved up into his rightful position to cover A's cross-court attempt. B must move back out of the way, but is ready to return to the front to cover after team C-D shoots. C has moved into her coverage position in the middle and will cover the kill attempt into the right corner or the pass down the right wall.

If the serve goes to C in the right alley, then just reverse the service-return options described on pages 163-164, and reverse the responsibilities of A, B, and D. Once again, B must be ready to retreat into the back left corner for a ceiling ball.

The Volley

Just as in singles, the volley should be used extensively in doubles because it will allow your team to hold a center-court position. (Remember the general rule: if the ball comes at waist level or below, cut it off on one bounce or volley it; if it comes higher than that, take it off the back wall.)

By volleying from center-court—in front of your opponents—you will have a greater offensive shot selection, and since your opponents are not in their optimum coverage positions, a ball killed a little higher than normal has a good chance of going for a winner. Conversely, when you let a hard-driven ball go by at waist level or below, then your opponents can return to their ideal defensive positions as you retreat towards the back wall. You will be forced to virtually "roll-out" your kill attempt.

The Overhead Drive and Kill

Both of these shots can be used effectively in doubles. If you find an opponent lagging back, use the overhead kill to try to end the rally or to force him forward. If you find an opponent a little too far forward, use the overhead drive to force the ball to bounce up into his chest area for a difficult return.

The Ceiling Ball

Doubles can sometimes turn into long ceiling ball rallies. If your team doesn't want to play that type of deliberate game, you must change the pace with an overhead kill or an overhead drive. And any time an opponent's ceiling ball comes up short, or goes long off the back wall, be ready to set up for a kill attempt or passing shot.

The ceiling ball, of course, will have good strategic value when your opponents control center-court and you don't want to risk a kill or pass attempt. In which case you'll try to drive them back with a ceiling shot.

THE IMPORTANCE OF CENTER COURT

Center-court control is a must for winning doubles.

First, if your team is in the center court, you are in a better position to cover your opponent's different scoring attempts.

Second, you are shooting from closer to the front wall and should be more accurate with your shots.

When a player (B in this photograph) is hitting from the middle of the court during a rally, here are his options: (1) pinch the ball into the left corner—or his nearest front corner—away from D; (2) cross-court the ball by C.

Three players can play a game called "cutthroat," in which one person plays against a doubles team for as long as he or she can retain the serve. The server can hit the ball to either opponent and regular racquetball rules are followed. The serve rotates among the three players until one person reaches 21 points. Obviously, the server must direct the ball into a back corner so that he or she can relocate properly in center court. Thereafter, the premium is put on his or her ability to anticipate and to cut off or volley balls coming off the front wall waist-high or lower.

Third, it's much easier to see the ball if you're standing in front of opponents.

Fourth, you can use a wider variety of kills and pinches into the front wall because you don't have to shoot around other players.

COMMUNICATION

Good communication is mandatory if your team hopes to maximize its ability. This communication should start before the match begins and should carry through to a critique of the completed match.

The pre-game discussion should include the tactics you'll be using in your coverage, your offensive and defensive shots, and the types of serves that will be effective against your opponents. Don't be closed-minded. Reverse your thinking and try to answer these same questions about your own team so that you might anticipate your opponents' attack. Also decide on the verbal signals (i.e., "yours, mine") you'll give each other on questionable balls that come between you.

Each team is allowed 3 time-outs a game (30 to 60 seconds long) and you should use this time not just to towel off and catch your breath, but to talk strategy. The team that makes sensible adjustments during time-outs—such as by changing its shot selection—can often slow the other team's momentum and gain the offensive. There's nothing more satisfying than to win a match because of adjustments like these.

Often times the pace and pressure is so hectic in doubles that when the actual match is over, you are physically and mentally relieved. But it's best if you and your teammate can take a little time to analyze your performance. Remember, you want to learn from all your matches.

GLOSSARY

Ace serve: when the serve takes 2 bounces before the opponent can return the ball to the front wall; usually occurs on the low-drive and hard "Z" serves.

Anticipation: the physical and mental preparation you should use in predicting what type of shot your opponent will hit.

Around-the-wall-ball: defensive shot that first hits high on the side wall, then the front wall, and then rebounds in the air to the other side wall before finally striking the floor at two-thirds court.

Avoidable hinder: a hinder or interference, not necessarily intentional, which clearly hampers the continuance of a rally; results in a loss of serve or point in tournament play.

Ceiling shot: the best percentage defensive shot; ball hits the ceiling 0 to 3 feet from front wall, bounces near service zone, and locates in deep court.

Center court: the area directly behind the back service line (approximately 14 feet wide by 11 feet deep) where most balls funnel during typical racquetball play.

Cocked wrist position: the position of the wrist when the racquet is pulled back in its set position.

Crack ball: shot that strikes the juncture of the side or rear wall and the floor; ball squirts out irretrievably.

Cross-court pass: a shot that strikes the front wall at such an angle that it goes by your opponent and heads for the opposite back corner of the court.

Cutthroat: racquetball game with 3 players. Each player, during his serve, plays against and scores points against the other 2 players. The first player to get 21 points wins.

Cutting off the ball: hitting the ball as it comes to you on one bounce, normally when you are in center court and you don't want the ball to get past you.

Defensive shot: a shot hit when you don't have an offensive opportunity, and whose purpose is to prolong the rally until you get an offensive shot.

Diagonal kill shot: a risky kill attempt hit diagonally into the opposite front corner. It goes for a winner when hit properly, but when missed it comes right back to center court for a setup.

Die in the back corner: slang term for a ball that takes its second bounce in the back corners of the court.

Down-the-wall shot: a ball that hits the front wall and then travels parallel to a side wall toward the back corner—without hitting the side wall, and without rebounding off the back wall (also known as a down-the-line shot).

Flail: slang term for putting your entire body into your shot.

Freak ball: when the ball takes an unexpected carom off the walls.

Half-lob serve: ball hit with medium speed that carries just past the back service line and does not come off the back wall.

High-lob serve: ball touches the side wall on its descent into the back court but does not come off the back wall.

Hitting alley: the lane the ball travels on its way to the front wall.

Kill: shot that hits low on the front wall and rebounds with so little bounce that a legal return is impossible.

Long serve: an illegal serve that hits the back wall in the air before it touches the floor.

Low-drive serve: ball that hits the front wall with force and then angles quickly into the back corners.

Offensive shot: a shot whose objective is to win the rally (*i.e.,* the kill or pass).

Open-stance swing: the type of stance most often used in center court when the ball comes quickly.

Pinch: kill shot that angles low off the front wall and one side wall, in either sequence; most effective when hit within a 2-foot range of the front corner.

Plum shot: an easy setup. You should always go for a kill attempt when you have this opportunity.

Quick racquet: the ability to swing your racquet through the ball very fast; used most often in center-court play.

Ready position: the body position you use to await your opponent's next shot. This same position is used in returning serving.

Reflex swing: used when the ball comes quickly into center court and forces you to react instinctively as you swing at the ball.

Roll-out: the perfect kill shot, in which the ball strikes the front wall so close to the floor that it rebounds with no bounce and rolls along the floor.

Screen serve: when the ball comes too close to the server's body on its way back from the front wall; usually happens only on the low-drive serve.

Service box: an area 18 inches wide on each end of the service zone, for use in doubles. The partner of the server must stand in this box until the served ball passes the back service line.

Service zone: the area between the service line and the short line (5 feet deep) and extending to both side walls, from where the serve must be hit.

Short serve: an illegal serve that fails to carry over the back service line (the short line) before it touches the floor.

Shot into the back wall: the last and most desperate way to return the ball to the front wall.

Skip ball: ball that hits the floor before reaching the front wall.

Soft shot: a softly struck ball, usually used to return a retrievable kill shot, and aimed low into the front wall.

Straight-in kill: a shot that strikes and rebounds directly off the front wall, with no side-wall contact; also known as a front-wall kill.

Time out: Each player is allowed 3 per game and 2 in a tie-breaker. The length is usually 30 to 60 seconds.

Unavoidable or regular hinder: an interference of normal play brought about unintentionally or uncontrollably by the players, the court, the equipment, or other hindrances.

Volley: a ball hit directly on the rebound from the front wall before it contacts the floor; known by many as the fly-kill attempt.

Wallpaper shot: a shot that hugs a side wall so closely that it is difficult to return.

Winner: a shot that ends the point or wins the rally outright; any ball that bounces twice in any area of the court before your opponent can retrieve it.

Z-ball: Considered a defensive shot by most, this ball hits high up on the front wall in either corner, ricochets quickly into the nearest side wall, then travels to the opposite side wall before finally striking the floor.

Z-serve: a ball that hits the front wall about head-high in the front corner, then angles diagonally into the opposite back corner and does not come off the back wall.